Painting Paradise

The Art of Ting Shao Kuang

CHINA BOOKS
& Periodicals, Inc.

SAN·FRANCISCO

Book and cover design by Linda Revel
Edited by Ma Baolin

First Edition 1998

Library of Congress Catalog Card Number: 98-071291
ISBN (Paperback) 0-8351-2638-2
ISBN (Hardcover) 0-8351-2637-4

Printed in Hong Kong

CHINA
BOOKS
& Periodicals, Inc.

(Left to right) Annabelle Weiner, Deputy Secretary General, WFUNA; Boutros Boutros-Ghali, Secretary-General of the United Nations; Ting Shao Kuang; Anthony Fouracre, Chief, United Nations Postal Administration

TABLE OF CONTENTS

PREFACE

THIS BOOK WAS WRITTEN with the help of many friends. I would like to thank them all. The artists I met in China and in the United States were each one very kind and helpful. My life is much richer for my association with them. Many thanks to the artists Liu Bingjiang, Zhou Ling, Zhong Shuheng, Liu Jude, Situ Jie, He Neng, He Deguang, Zhang Ding, Yuan Yunfu, Wu Guanzhong, Yao Zhonghua, Huang Yongyu, Zhang Shiyan, Zhu Naizhen, Pang Tao, Lin Gang, and their families for their hospitality and stimulating conversation. Others in China who were very helpful include relatives of Ting Shao Kuang, especially his nephew, Ding Yi; Pang Xunqin's widow, Yuan Yunyi; Mrs. Winnie Lau Yoshimura; Mrs. Wang Yuying; and Robin and Tim Stratford. I appreciate the generosity of He Neng and He Deguang, who lent me valuable journals and historical materials from their own collections. I would also like to thank Dr. Luo Kongxiong for allowing me to view paintings by artists from Yunnan in his private collection. Zhang Wen-kuang, Charles Liu and Josephine Arnold assisted me in the translation of taped conversations with artists. Charles Liu also facilitated meetings with Ting Shao Kuang and helped me in many other ways. Steve Thole at Miami University patiently advised me on the use of WordPerfect. I owe thanks to the artist himself, for the generous amounts of time he spent with me, and to his family. His mother, his brother, Peter Ting, his daughter, Angelina Ting, and his former wife, Zhang Daxi, were all especially helpful. My husband and children deserve the most praise, for they endured both my absence during long research trips and my presence during the stressful months of writing. This book is dedicated to them.

CHAPTER ONE

THE EARLY YEARS (1939–1962)

TING SHAO KUANG [Ding Shaoguang] was born on October 7, 1939 during the Sino-Japanese War as his family fled occupied territories and moved westward. He was born in Shaanxi Province in Hanzhong, Chenggu County, the fourth child of Ting Chün-sheng [Ding Junsheng, also known as Johnson Ting, b.1903] and Lee Hsiang-chü [Li Xiangju, b.1915].[1] A month later his family moved to Xi'an where his father served in the regional office of the Kuomintang. The family lived in Xi'an for seven years, until the war ended and the Kuomintang office where Ting Chün-sheng served was moved to Beijing.

In 1948 Ting Chün-sheng was elected to the Kuomintang Parliament and left Beijing to meet with other officials in Nanjing. Since he was to be gone for two months, his wife joined him in the south. She left the four oldest children, including Shao Kuang, at home with her parents in Beijing to attend school but took the two youngest children with her. They arrived in Nanjing in October only to discover that the Kuomintang position in the south was deteriorating rapidly in the face of Communist opposition. In December Ting Chün-sheng left suddenly for Taiwan. Lee Hsiang-chü and their two children soon followed by train to Shanghai, then by boat to the island.

According to Shao Kuang's mother, the evacuation was seen as temporary. At the time she did not know that it would be more than thirty years before she would see her four older children again. Ting Chün-sheng died in Taipei in 1979, less than a year before Shao Kuang and his mother were reunited in California.

In Taiwan Ting Chün-sheng continued as a member of the Kuomintang Parliament and as a Bureaucratic Investigator *(jianchayuan)* in the Nationalist government. His work in the judiciary branch, to which he was reelected each term for 35 years, involved the investigation of cases of bribery, including major cases dealing with the export of bananas to Japan. According to his son Peter Ting [Ding Shaoxiong], he was a kind, fair and gentle man who was never angry with his children and did not argue with his wife. He was not wealthy because he never accepted bribes, but he had many friends. Thousands attended his funeral, and Chiang Chingkuo wrote his memorial script.[2]

Lee Hsiang-chü gave birth to one more child and turned to Buddhism for comfort after the separation from her four children in Beijing. The estranged family maintained contact with one another through a friend in Hong Kong until the death of that friend in 1965. When Shirley

Ting Hu [Ding Shaoyun], a graduate of Taiwan University, moved to the United States in 1978, she tried to reestablish contact with her older brothers and sister, but no one was at the old address in Beijing, and her letters were returned. Then in 1979, Ting Shao Kuang's art was reviewed in a Hong Kong newspaper; friends forwarded the information to his mother in Taiwan only months after the death of his father.

Ting Shao Kuang's maternal grandparents owned a large house and four acres of land in Beijing. Six months after Mao Zedong entered the city, the children and their grandparents were removed from their home and placed in a tiny apartment without furniture. The boy used a door for a bed. Abandoned by his parents and reduced to poverty at the age of nine, Ting was also the victim of cruel teasing by neighborhood children. To cope with the situation, the once quiet and cooperative boy became fiercely aggressive. For about four years he fought with older children, learning martial arts to defend himself, and joined a street gang for protection. He even took part in small-scale vandalism, climbing on the roofs of people's houses and shooting at glass windows with a slingshot. He performed daring physical feats in front of his friends and sometimes hurt himself.

Around the age of ten he began to read classical Chinese stories, such as *The Water Margin* and *The Romance of the Three Kingdoms*. Later his oldest brother introduced him to Western literature in translation, and Ting read Tolstoy and Balzac at night instead of sleeping. He gave up his fierce outdoor play for reading and determined that one day he would become an author.

Ting Shao Kuang's oldest brother, Ding Shaozeng, who was nearly 18 when his parents left for Taiwan, embraced Communism and joined the party but was expelled as a Rightist during the 1957 Anti-Rightist Campaign. For six years he performed manual labor and suffered many indignities as the son of a former Kuomintang official. Ding Shaozeng is now a professor of mathematics at the Xi'an Transportation Institute. Because of his own early education and literary interests he was able to influence his younger brother's taste in literature. From that point the young artist-to-be began his lifelong pursuit of learning from books..

Ting began to paint when he was eleven, and received his first formal training under Lei Jiannong at the Beijing Number Eight High School in 1954. During lunch hours the youth would take something to eat to Lei's home and practice drawing from plaster casts that Lei kept there. Ting remembers that the walls of Lei's small room were covered with black cloth and that very little light was allowed into the room. Lei taught his students the importance of line and showed them how to use line continuously without stopping.

It was at Beijing Number Eight High School that Ting found his first soul-mate and formed an important friendship with the talented artist Liu Bingjiang (b.1937). Both of them took art, and themselves, very seriously. After finishing their homework they would often take walks in the evening and discuss their ideas about art.[3] Soviet-style academic realism dominated the teaching methods at their school, and they wondered together if it was really the kind of art that could inspire them. Though they were unfamiliar with most Western art, they were attracted to what little they knew of the outside world, and they looked to the West for artistic quality.

In 1955 the Central Academy of Fine Arts (*Zhongyang Meishu Xueyuan*) established a high school for gifted art students,[4] and Ting Shao Kuang was admitted into the first class of students to attend. Many of the professors at the Academy also taught classes at the high school. Ting's teachers there included Dong Xiwen (1914–1973), a member of a group of artists who copied mural paintings at Dunhuang between 1943 and 1945, and Wang Shike.

Siquieros's Visit to China

In October 1955 the Mexican muralist and secretary of the Mexican Communist party David Alfaro Siquieros (1896–1974) stopped in Beijing after a visit to the Soviet Union. His profound appreciation of Chinese sculptures and ancient murals impressed not only Ting Shao Kuang, but a number of established artists as well, especially those at the Central Academy of Arts and Crafts (*Zhongyang Gongyimeishu Xueyuan*). One anecdote about Siquieros's visit that circulates among Beijing artists reveals why Siquieros had such an impact. Siquieros was taken by party officials in China to see the Buddhist caves at Yungang. When he confronted the great Buddha there he knelt in awe. Although as a Communist he was antireligious, he claimed that in the presence of such a significant expression of the Chinese culture, he could not possibly stand. The attending officials were also compelled to kneel. For Ting Shao Kuang this story both reinforced his pride in his cultural heritage and poked fun at Chinese officials who lacked respect for the ancient art of China.

"Siquieros had a tremendous impact on me when I was young," Ting said. "I was especially influenced by his thoughts."[5] After his visit to China, Siquieros wrote an open letter to Chinese artists that was published in the Central Academy of Fine Arts newsletter in 1956. Both the original letter, which some professors at the Central

Academy of Fine Arts had seen, and the revised version published in the newsletter were the subject of much discourse among artists in Beijing. The young and impressionable Ting began to gain a heady sense of his own direction as he listened to the debates. In the letter Siquieros criticized the academic realism of Russian art as art that had no life. He was especially critical of the Chinese for training their artists according to the Russian school, in which they learned to draw by copying Greek and Roman plaster casts and ignored their own 5000-year-old culture. Siquieros rejected European models for his own mural paintings and looked to Pre-Columbian art and the Mexican people for style and subject matter. He believed Chinese artists should also explore their own cultural past and let the art of their own people inspire their works.

In the spring of 1956, a few months after Siquieros' visit, an exhibit of Mexican graphic art was shown in Beijing. Photographs of the famous murals by Rivera, Orozco, and Siquieros were also part of the show. The exhibit was reviewed extensively in Beijing newspapers, and Mexican artists were praised for speaking "with the voice of the Mexican people," for expressing "their heroic, militant and selfless spirit."[6] This was the first and only meaningful exhibit of foreign works that Ting was able to see in China. Although the works of some French artists, including his future favorites Picasso and Matisse, were also shown in Beijing in 1956, Ting heard nothing about that show, which presumably was not open to impressionable students.[7]

Ting witnessed another influential exhibit in Beijing in October 1955 made up of copies of murals in the Buddhist Mogao cave temples near Dunhuang, along the ancient Silk Road in the northwestern province of Gansu.[8] During the Second World War Zhang Daqian (1899–1983) led a team of artists who made replicas of wall paintings that were created primarily between the third and the eighth centuries. They were shown once in Chengdu in Sichuan province in 1944, then resurfaced for the show in Beijing. Ting's interest in the form and color of the paintings was captured early, and he visited the caves himself in 1967, absorbing impressions that would inform his later style.

Central Academy of Arts and Crafts

After graduating from high school, Ting Shao Kuang did not apply for admission to the Central Academy of Fine Arts (CAFA) as his friends and teachers had expected. Instead he took the exams for the Central Academy of Arts and Crafts (CAAC). As a student at the CAFA-affiliated high school, Ting became disillusioned with the emphasis on politically correct art. The CAFA, under the leadership of Xu Beihong (1895–1953), had become the bastion for conservative Western methods in art. At that time, students learned the Russian socialist-realist style and applied it to figure paintings of government-sanctioned subjects. Siquieros had confirmed Ting's youthful distaste for academic realism, and Ting hoped that he would be able to learn more about twentieth-century Western art by studying under European-trained painters such as Pang Xunqin at the CAAC. At that point his ideas about art had not really matured, but he had a strong feeling of dissatisfaction with the kind of art that was issuing from the Soviet Union. Despite pressure from his friends, including Liu Bingjiang, he shunned the prestigious CAFA and sought guidance from teachers he knew at CAAC. He was especially attracted to Zhang Guangyu (1900–1965), an illustrator and traditional Chinese painter who taught classes at the CAFA while Ting was a student at the affiliated high school but who later transferred to the CAAC.

To gain acceptance to the CAAC Ting had to pass exams in several areas, including drawing, creativity, sculpture, and design. For the creativity exam students were given four hours to complete a painting on a specified subject. Ting's strength was his drawing, and he felt that his acceptance to the CAAC was based on that. Since the CAAC was a design school, he was also asked to design a pattern based on a flower as part of the entrance exam. He remembers that he was able to make a good painting of the flower, but not a good design. Despite his obvious preference for the fine arts over design, he was accepted at the school and pursued his studies in painting there under the direction of several remarkable painters who will be discussed below.

Ting began his studies at the CAAC in the fall of 1957. There were ten students in the new class, some from military families and some from the CAFA-affiliated high school. One of the military students, Zhang Shiyan (b.1938) from Shandong, became a close friend. "One thing we shared in common," said Zhang, "was that we stayed up at night and had lots of time to talk."[9] Ting shared his passion for literature with Zhang, and they pored over the translated works of Jack London, as well as his biography, discussing the ideas that London set forth in his books. They also admired the works of the French novelist Romain Rolland and compared their own lives to that of his famous character, Jean Christophe, who as a young man suffered many hardships. His eventual success through hard work gave them spiritual comfort.[10]

Ting was known among his fellow students for his passionate approach to art. He thoroughly explored each new kind of art that he learned about, then cast it aside for another new approach, which he explored just as thoroughly. He was genuine, frank, and completely loyal to his friends, often going out of his way to help others. His level of energy was high, so that he was able to spend longer hours working on his art than his peers. He was also something of a ringleader, introducing new discoveries about Western art he had made in the library to other students.

Although Ting Shao Kuang sought more freedom by choosing to study at the CAAC, his formal classes were still confined primarily to the socialist-realist methods imported from the Soviet Union. What he learned of twentieth-century Western art came primarily from his own study of art books in the library. During his third year of undergraduate study he came across paintings by Picasso and Matisse in the Beijing library. It was the first time he had seen anything like their work and he became very excited about it. He spent hours in the library, enthusiastically studying Picasso's new viewpoint. Eventually the library reported to the CAAC that a *liumang* (hooligan) from their school was reading unhealthy material at the library. When Zhang Ding (b.1919) heard about the report he was very interested. "I'll handle this one," he said. "I'll be the one to criticize him."[11] Zhang Ding invited Ting to his home, and rather than reprimand him, congratulated him and gave him his own library card with which to borrow the subversive material. That experience was the beginning of a fast friendship between Zhang Ding and Ting Shao Kuang.

Ting borrowed the books on Picasso first and spent many hours copying the reproductions, trying to see things from Picasso's perspective. Ting said:

> At first it was direct copying, but at the end it was not. I just painted what I felt. I loved Picasso and my works looked a lot like his. I used various methods and materials, including plaster board, which gives a very intense color. I used knives and nails to make lines, cutting through the color so that white lines appeared on the board. I can still do that—it's very beautiful.[12]

When Ting had exhausted Picasso he turned to other early twentieth-century Western artists—Modigliani, Matisse, Miro, Klee, Dubuffet, and Dali, all of whom influenced his thoughts about painting. In addition to the European masters he also studied the Mexican mural painters Rivera, Orozco, and Siquieros, whose photographed works he had seen on exhibit in Beijing in 1956. "As I studied the history of Western art my attention became riveted on the mural painting," he explained.[13]

During that period Ting did many paintings, and some of the younger students at the CAAC began to emulate him. His irrepressible enthusiasm for modern European masters was well known to the other students, and before long he was reported by one of them to the Ministry of Culture. In response the Ministry of Culture sent a letter to all the art institutions in China, claiming that the CAAC was spreading bourgeois culture and warning them to avoid this particular evil. It was 1960, and the CAAC was severely criticized and reprimanded for allowing young students to study foreign bourgeois artists.

According to Ting, the teachers at the CAAC were secretly pleased with his enthusiasm for Picasso and tolerated his introduction of French artists to the other students. But the teachers themselves were unable to discuss these modern artists or give evidence of their influence on their own works. Ting was relatively undisturbed by the criticism and largely ignored it. But he knew that he had caused trouble for his teachers.

Zhang Guangyu (1900–1965)

Zhang Guangyu and Pang Xunqin were the two professors at the the CAAC who most deeply influenced Ting Shao Kuang. Zhang Guangyu graduated from the Shanghai Art Academy where he studied modern painting under Zhang Yuguang,[14] as well as traditional Chinese painting and theater set design. Later he studied Peking Opera, and the combination of literature, dance, and the decorative art of Chinese opera had an important impact on the development of his style.[15] From 1921–28 he worked as an advertising designer for a cigarette company. His knowledge of Peking Opera led to an interest in the folk art of China and while he worked as an advertiser he studied traditional Chinese crafts, including the anonymous arts of ancient China—decorative bricks, Buddhist sculpture, and temple murals.

During the Sino-Japanese war Zhang worked as an illustrator, producing anti-Japanese cartoons for various newspapers, and was forced to move inland as the Japanese overran the coastal cities. As the war progressed he began to satirize the corruption and mismanagement of the Nationalist government. Unable to openly criticize the Kuomintang, he masked his political satire in depictions of recognizable figures from history and classical literature. One of the best examples of his political satire is a series of drawings based on Journey to the West (*Xi you ji*), that was exhibited in Chengdu in the 1940s. In this series Monkey represented the Chinese people, while the multitudinous demons and monsters who tried to defeat him on his journey were thinly disguised representations of corrupt officials.[16] The drawings won an international award and were used as the basis for the popular movie Journey to the West.[17]

At the end of the war Zhang moved to Hong Kong and continued work as an illustrator. In 1949 he was invited to return to Beijing as a professor at the CAFA. When the CAAC was established, he joined the faculty there. During the Anti-Rightist Campaign of 1957 he was criticized for formalism (*xing shi zhu yi*), or creating paintings concerned with aestheticism rather than didacticism, though he escaped being branded a Rightist.

Zhang's influence on Ting was both stylistic and theoretical. During the 1930s he had studied folk art and minority cultures in southwestern China. While artists such as Pang Xunqin, Lin Fengmian and Xu Beihong looked at Chinese art with new eyes after studying in Europe, Zhang

began to look at the long tradition of Chinese art from the point of view of the anonymous art of the people, and he also saw Chinese art with new eyes. He taught Ting and other students to look beyond the literati tradition of painting, to consider the rich tradition of sculpture and colorful murals that was also an important part of China's art. He warned them not to limit themselves to learning only the brush strokes of *wenrenhua* (literati painting), but to look beyond those narrow confines to the magnificent panorama of decorative motifs on bronzes, ceramics, architectural bricks, and temple walls. Siquieros's exhortation to Chinese artists to look to their native past for inspiration was well received by Zhang, as it had been his practice to do just that since the 1920s.

It might be surmised that Zhang's enthusiasm for folk art—the art of the people—was political in nature, as he was not unsympathetic to the Communist cause during the 1930s. But Ting argues that Zhang did not study folk art from a political point of view, as encouraged by Mao Zedong in his 1942 talks on art and literature at Yan'an, but rather from an artistic point of view, like Picasso's study of African masks. He points out that artists were interested in both folk art and minority cultures long before 1942, and that Mao's ideas about art were not especially original.[18] While Zhang's interest in folk art was probably apolitical, it is possible that his aesthetic investigation of ancient art and folk crafts was also inspired in some degree by nationalism.

Ting Shao Kuang remembers vividly the new approach to Chinese art taught by Zhang Guangyu in art history classes at the CAAC. Always eager to study something new, he followed Zhang's example, turning to ancient Chinese art and the folk art of China's minorities to discover motifs that could be used in his own work. This visual and theoretical orientation is perhaps the most captivating aspect of Ting's work today, for which he owes an important debt to his teacher. Zhang Guangyu also encouraged Ting to travel to Yunnan province to gather material for his graduation project. His role bringing about this turning point in Ting's life will be discussed later in this chapter.

Ting is also stylistically and technically indebted to Zhang Guangyu. While he has far surpassed his teacher in his masterful use of sinuous line, it was Zhang Guangyu who taught Ting the importance of line. As an illustrator, Zhang used line alone to convey his message. Although Ting is a painter, he mastered line thoroughly before he added color to his works. His first important works were *baihua*, a form composed entirely of even black lines. Ting said,

> Zhang Guangyu taught me a very simple principle:
> There are only two lines. One is vertical and the
> other is horizontal. The horizontal line can express

tranquility and death. The vertical line is the symbol of life. The vertical line is variable, and when one puts two lines together there is change. Parallel horizontal lines do not express change. This is very simple, but in an actual painting it is more complicated. I use a lot of parallel horizontal lines in my paintings. That's why there is a quiet feeling in them. I learned that from Zhang Guangyu.[19]

The illustrations for a Dai story from Yunnan—*The Peacock Maiden*, commissioned for a folklore series by the People's Literature Press in the early 1950s—are a good example of Zhang's stylistic influence on Ting. The story recounts Prince Zhaoshutun's search for a wife who was not only beautiful but also clever. He falls in love with the youngest of seven peacock maidens, and like other folk heroes, proves his worthiness of her with feats of valor impossible for an ordinary human.[20] The roots of Ting's exquisitely patterned backgrounds can be seen in the stylized pattern of the peacock cloak held by Zhaoshutun and the flowering tree he hangs it on **(Fig. 4a)**, and in the flat, geometric representation of the peacock feathers worn by Nanmarouna as she flies away from the executioner's block **(Fig. 4b)**. The repetition of a stylized motif can also be seen in the rush of air beneath Nanmarouna, in the wooden block from which she flies, in her bodice, in the roof of the castle, and even in the sun and the mountains behind her. While Zhang Guangyu's patterns are simple and unpretentious, Ting Shao Kuang has developed the decorative patterns in his own works with intricate and stunning detail.

One can also see a connection between the fine lines of the giant bird feathers drawn by Zhang **(Fig. 4e)** and Ting's masterful ink representations of the lush tropical forest of Xishuangbanna **(Fig. 5)**. The feathery lines of the palm fronds on the left and the ferns on the right echo the unusual and highly imaginative illustration of Zhaoshutun climbing into the quill of the giant bird that would carry him to the kingdom of Mengwodongban.

While Zhang Guangyu's depictions of the beautiful peacock princess herself **(Figs. 4b, 4f)** may not have influenced Ting's current depictions of women, it is nonetheless important to point out that Ting was romantically moved by the story itself, as were countless other Chinese who read it and saw Zhang's illustrations. Years later he used the story as the theme for one of his paintings, *The Peacock Princess* **(Fig. 50)**.

It is significant that one of Ting Shao Kuang's most influential teachers was an illustrator. Zhang Guangyu's illustrations of literature were naturally attractive to a young man who had found meaning and sustenance in great works of classical Chinese and Western literature, and they struck a romantic chord within Ting. As an illustrator Zhang was also in a position to teach Ting the technical aspects of line and to show him that line was an expressive medium in and of itself.

The importance of Zhang Guangyu's influence on Ting Shao Kuang is significant, but his contributions to art education in China in general also should not be overlooked. His ideas about folk art and the art of China's past influenced a generation of students studying at the CAAC; a number of China's most prominent artists, including Zhang Ding and Huang Yongyu (b. 1924), revere him as their teacher. He and his colleagues at the CAAC also helped develop an artistic approach in direct opposition to that of proponents of academic realism at the CAFA. This conflict between faculties at the two institutions is one reason for Zhang Guangyu's continuing relative obscurity in the West. Xu Beihong, the first president of the CAFA, despised modern European art. He was in a position to discriminate in hiring against artists who were interested in contemporary masters like Picasso and Matisse. Professors who championed contemporary European art or who opposed the method of academic realism were relegated to teaching positions at the CAAC. When Western art historians began visiting China again during the 1980s they were introduced first to artists at the politically more prestigious CAFA. Thus our picture of the development of twentieth-century Chinese art is at this point still fragmented.

Pang Xunqin (1906–1983)

According to Pang Xunqin's second wife, Yuan Yunyi, Ting Shao Kuang was not only a leader among his peers, but also a favorite among the teachers at the CAAC.[21]

Despite Pang Xunqin's political difficulties at the time Ting entered school, Ting respected and admired the older painter, and they became friends. Pang was attracted by young Ting's talent and enthusiasm, as well as his honest and forthright character. In 1956 Pang was assigned by the State Council, under the direction of Zhou Enlai, to head the newly formed Central Academy of Arts and Crafts. Because Pang was not a Communist Party member he was given the title of Vice-Director of the academy, rather than President, but he was in fact the person in charge. During the summer of 1957 he was persecuted as a Rightist, along with other prominent men in the art world, Jiang Feng (1910–1982), vice-chairman of the Chinese Artists' Association, and Xu Yansun, director of the new Beijing Academy of Chinese Painting.[22] Demoted in rank, he remained at the CAAC. It was at this point in Pang's career, the fall of 1957, that Ting became the student of this influential teacher. That Ting embraced Pang's ideas and friendship despite his political problems is indicative of the independent spirit of Ting Shao Kuang.

Pang Xunqin, originally from Jiangsu Province, went to Paris in 1925 but returned to China in 1928 when a prominent French critic described his work as technically proficient but lacking any expression of his Chinese heritage. According to one source, Pang burned all his works before leaving Paris so that he could start afresh in China.[23] Interestingly, Ting Shao Kuang himself frequently burned paintings in the 1960s and 1970s, partly to escape criticism, but just as often because of dissatisfaction with his work.

Pang returned to his family home in the country, and from there went to Shanghai where he organized a society of repatriated painters who shared an interest in cubism, fauvism, and other modern French art movements. Called Société des Deux Mondes, the group met from 1929 to 1932. Then in 1932, in response to Lu Xun's call for artists to depict real people (meaning the proletariat) and their struggles, Pang organized another group with very different aims. With Ni Yide (b.1902), a professor at the Shanghai Academy, he formed the Storm Society (Juelan She). Where the Société des Deux Mondes had promoted a type of art that was not easily understood and therefore inaccessible to all but a small group of intellectuals, this society was dedicated to reaching the people through its art. Juelan She continued until 1935.[24] Pang supported himself in Shanghai from 1929 to 1935 from his own studio, where he both taught painting and sold his works.

During the Sino-Japanese War Pang Xunqin served with other refugee artists in a variety of significant jobs in western China. He worked in Kunming as a researcher for an art institute established by Academia Sinica to study minority art and the art of early China. He was also employed jointly by the National Museum and Academia Sinica to collect embroidery and costumes of the Miao people in Guizhou. As a result of these labors, Pang Xunqin was one of the first artists whose works were influenced by the colorful handicrafts and exotic lifestyle of the border people. His study of early Chinese art also opened his eyes to the possibility of a new kind of art history: art history without names. Like Zhang Guangyu, Pang Xunqin would later pass on these new ideas to his most receptive student, Ting Shao Kuang. Pang also worked in Chengdu as a teacher at the Sichuan Provincial Art College, and it was there in 1944 that he formed yet another art society.[25] Pang's compulsion for organizing other artists into supportive groups during periods of hardship was probably related to his experiences in France, where bohemian groups, giddy with new ideas about art and society, flourished in the 1920s. It is most likely that romantic stories of these societies were passed on to his students; Ting fashioned his own group of artists who met secretly during the Cultural Revolution, then organized formally into the art society called Shen She after Mao's death and the arrest of the Gang of Four.

Stylistically, Pang Xunqin influenced Ting Shao Kuang less than did Zhang Guangyu. The painting he did after his return to China includes a series of dancers based on his

research on early China, landscapes in both oil and Western watercolor such as the one shown in **Figure 6**, a few portraits, and romantic depictions of minority figures.[26] When the Cultural Revolution began he retired and after that painted primarily vases of flowers in the western still-life mode.[27] It is only in his seductive portrayals of Miao women that one glimpses the romantic spirit that also inhabits the paintings of Ting Shao Kuang.

As with Zhang Guangyu, relatively little about Pang Xunqin has been published in the West. His contributions to art education in the early years of the People's Republic of China are significant, however, and should be more widely known. As head of the CAAC he devoted more of his time to his students than to his own works. Pang promoted the study of folk art and the study of the history of Chinese art from a different point of view. His early and continuous rivalry with Xu Beihong[28] sometimes put him at a disadvantage in the politically charged art arena, but he guided the CAAC through the perils of the Anti-Rightist campaign to a prominent position in China. Pang recruited talented artists such as Zhang Ding, Wu Guanzhong, and Yuan Yunfu to teach painting at the CAAC and gained for the CAAC the reputation of being less conservative than the CAFA. In the school of design, the most prominent department at the CAAC, he was an innovator, basing his art on historical research and pulling design elements from traditional Chinese decorative arts. Pang taught this way of looking at the past to Ting Shao Kuang who used it effectively many years later in his paintings.

Zhang Ding (b.1917)

Besides Zhang Guangyu and Pang Xunqin, two other professors at the CAAC, Zhang Ding and Yuan Yunfu, have had a significant impact in the life of Ting Shao Kuang. In her book Yunnan School: A Renaissance in Chinese Painting, Joan Lebold Cohen describes Ting Shao Kuang as the protégé of Zhang Ding.[29] In fact, Zhang Ding himself remembers Ting as his favorite student during the period he studied at the CAAC (1957–1962).[30] A loyal Communist Party member despite criticism of his art as early as the 1930s, Zhang Ding attended the Yan'an Forum on Arts and Literature in 1942 and was active in the Party's fight against the Nationalists from the 1920s until its victory in 1949.[31] He was well known for his political cartoons satirizing both the Japanese and the Kuomintang. When the CAAC was founded in 1956, Zhang was first appointed chairman of the department of applied art, then soon after became chairman of the Chinese painting department. During the Hundred Flowers Campaign of 1956–57, Zhang Ding criticized his contemporaries' reliance on Soviet art models and advocated the modernization of traditional Chinese painting. In the political atmosphere of deteriorating relations with the Soviet Union and an increasing emphasis on nationalism and self-reliance, Zhang's ideas gained temporary endorsement, and he enjoyed a brief period of prestige before the terrors of the Cultural Revolution. He rose to the position of vice-president of the CAAC and was able to facilitate Chinese art exhibitions in foreign countries.

As an official representative of China's art community, Zhang had the opportunity to meet Picasso in France in 1958. This event held almost mythical importance for his student, Ting Shao Kuang. After his own discovery of Picasso's work in the Beijing Library, Ting was enormously impressed by the fact that Zhang Ding had recently met him in Paris and to this day treasures a tiny photograph of his teacher with Picasso given him by Zhang Ding **(Fig. 7)**. He loves to tell a story about the gift that Zhang Ding gave to Picasso. According to Ting, the Chinese government prepared an elaborately carved ivory boat for Zhang Ding to take to Paris as a gift for the famous artist. Sensing that the gift was not appropriate, Zhang Ding let Guan Shanyue present the boat to Picasso, while he himself offered an inexpensive New Year's print (nianhua) he had purchased in a street market that depicted China's colorful door gods. Picasso was clearly more delighted with this humble gift than with the expensive ivory carving. Ting's enjoyment in retelling this story derives partly from its folkloric quality—the ordinary person gets the better of the government leaders who prepared the more elaborate gift. It also underscores his preference for the colorful and straightforward expression of Chinese folk art.

Zhang Ding suffered enormously during the Cultural Revolution, but after his rehabilitation in 1979 he was given a commission of major importance, the decoration of the Beijing airport. At that time he was able to call on former students throughout China, including Ting Shao Kuang, and bring them to Beijing to participate in what was to become a significant wall painting (bihua) movement that is still alive in China today. His plight during the Cultural Revolution will be discussed in Chapter Two, while his leadership role in the wall painting movement will be discussed in Chapter Four. In addition to the honors attendant on receiving this commission, Zhang was appointed President of the CAAC in 1981.

An Ancient Tower in Suzhou **(Fig. 8)** is an example of Zhang Ding's work in the 1950s, while Ting Shao Kuang was his student. Though politically motivated cartoons and wall paintings were his specialty, Zhang also loved traditional Chinese painting. This work employs the brush technique and the medium of traditional Chinese painting, ink on paper; however the composition and perspective are Western. Few of Zhang's paintings from this period survive, as most were destroyed by Red Guards during the Cultural Revolution.

In the late 1950s and early 1960s Zhang Ding took small groups of students on several short trips to Yunnan Province to sketch the landscape of Xishuangbanna. Ting saw the paintings that resulted from these exhibits, and when he traveled on his own in Yunnan in 1961–62 he occasionally joined Zhang Ding's group of students. While Ting absorbed Zhang Ding's interest in the scenery of this province, there is little evidence that Zhang Ding's style influenced Ting's own work, except that they both rendered the lush scenery of the tropical forest in monochrome ink. As Zhang Ding explained, Ting was more interested in the gongbi (finely detailed) style of Chinese painting, while he himself preferred xieyi (a freer, looser brush manner).[32]

Since his rehabilitation in 1979, Zhang Ding has continued his work in the area of traditional Chinese painting. He has also been commissioned to paint a number of panoramic landscapes to decorate hotels and public buildings, such as the colorful Sunrise at Xiyu Mountain **(Fig. 9)**, and a recently completed landscape for the controversial and beautiful new Bank of China in Hong Kong designed by I.M. Pei. His private works are monochrome ink landscapes painted on paper with jiaomo, a sticky black ink that is not mixed with water. Ancestral Home of the Mountain Spirit **(Fig. 10)**, for example, is a panoramic bird's-eye view of a vast expanse of complicated, twisted forms. The full, rich peaks are augmented by foliage and two small houses in the lower left, but it is the mountains that dominate the landscape and demonstrate the skilled and patient brushwork of the artist. Attached to the painting is a long inscription by a poet friend, combining the arts of painting and poetry in the manner of the literati painting of the past. The poem describes the poet's and Zhang Ding's journey to Tianzi Mountain just before the springtime Qing Ming festival, and the spiritual feelings that were evoked as they surveyed the mountains with their lingering snow. Pride in the motherland, the impetus for the revamping of traditional Chinese landscapes into majestic views that would stimulate nationalistic fervor for the Communist state, is common to both of these paintings. The public painting is simplified, however, and still retains the revolutionary color symbolism in its reddened peaks, while the private painting is more complex, documenting the artist's feelings.

Zhang Ding's mentoring had a powerful effect on Ting Shao Kuang while he was a student at the CAAC, both through his private encouragement of Ting's interest in modern European painters and his firsthand association with Picasso. Zhang's handling of the Beijing Library incident allowed Ting to pursue new artistic ideas. His own interest in painting the scenery of Yunnan province influenced Ting's enthusiasm for the area. And when politically observant professors at the CAAC objected to the westernized appearance of Ting's graduation piece, Zhang Ding's crucial support helped him override their objections and obtain his diploma.

Yuan Yunfu (b.1932)

One of the younger professors at the CAAC, Yuan Yunfu was also Ting Shao Kuang's teacher. A recent graduate of the Hangzhou Academy of Fine Arts, Yuan joined the faculty in 1956 when the academy was founded.[33] Yuan Yunfu remembers Ting as the most talented of the CAAC students and also as one who was different from his peers. His artistic temperament and his strong personality gave him the strength of will to explore his own avenues in art in spite of the conformist political climate. Ting paid no attention to politics, devoting himself entirely to the development of his art.[34] Yuan speculates that his ability at that time to disregard what was politically correct stemmed from the difficulties he had experienced as a child; Ting learned early to rely on himself and to ignore the criticism of others. Because of his frank and easy personality, he was able to get along with others well; perhaps his nonconformist ideas were not as objectionable as they might have been in a person with an abrasive personality. Yuan Yunfu also pointed out that Ting Shao Kuang belonged to two groups as a student: the teachers' group and the students' group. Because of his talent and respect for his teachers—even those in political trouble—he elicited the paternal attentions of Pang Xunqin, Zhang Guangyu and Zhang Ding, who treated him like a son and jointly introduced him to western art and art of the entire world. The younger Yuan Yunfu also became a friend and confidante of Ting Shao Kuang, and their friendship and professional relationship have continued through the many years that have passed since Ting was a student at the CAAC. Yuan Yunfu was another professor who shared an enthusiasm for the scenery of Xishuangbanna. He published an album of monochrome paintings of the area and, in 1978, helped Ting exhibit and publish his own monochrome paintings of Xishuangbanna in Beijing.

Yuan Yunfu introduced Ting Shao Kuang to his younger brother, Yuan Yunsheng (b. 1937), a student at the CAFA, and they became close friends. Through this friendship, and his friendship with Liu Bingjiang, Ting became influential among the students at the CAFA as well. He was a good speaker, attracting a gathering of students whenever he talked about the ideas he had learned from books and his professors, and in this way he gradually formulated his theories about art and life. Ting was popular among the other students—candid and easy-going, kind and sincere, and fiercely loyal to his friends. Often he remonstrated his friends if they were unkind to each other. Because of his high energy level, he not only had time for many friends, but he reportedly worked on his art sixteen hours a day, compared to the eight hours spent by most students.[35] In this way Ting Shao Kuang's years in school passed quickly and his early ideas about art took shape.

The Yellow River and Xishuangbanna

After three years of study at the CAAC, painting students had the opportunity to travel to an area of their choice in China and make sketches for their graduation project. The fourth year of study was to be spent "painting from life," a practice inspired by the increasing nationalism in China as it pulled away from the dominance of the Soviet Union. During the summer of his third year in college, Ting Shao Kuang decided to paint a large mural of the Yellow River. He wanted it to convey both the history of China and the history of its many art styles, progressing from realistic descriptions of nature to an expression of the beauty of his own feelings about art. But when he traveled to the Yellow River, he was so shocked by the devastating effects of the famine that plagued China following the failure of the Great Leap Forward in 1959 that he was unable to paint. Instead of symbolizing the source of China's greatness, the Yellow River had become an emblem of the nation's sickening failures. As he stared at the powerful river he imagined that he saw China's civilization come to a standstill, both artistically and culturally. First he saw the river running swiftly, and he interpreted this as a representation of the Han and Tang periods. As he stared at it longer and night began to fall, it seemed to him as though the river were thick, like mud—art and civilization slowing down during the Yuan period. Finally, when it was dark, the river seemed to harden into earth and stop moving, representing both social and artistic poverty and the cessation of all progress.

Unable to paint the Yellow River, Ting returned to Beijing where Huang Yongyu told him stories about his recent trip to Xishuangbanna in Yunnan Province. Ting Shao Kuang remembers this as the point at which he gave up all pretentions about painting something nationalistic and, despite the political climate, turned to "art for art's sake."[36]

He became very excited about the prospect of painting the exotic scenery and people of Xishuangbanna, and even imagined himself as kin to Gauguin, setting out on a tropical adventure. The experiences of his teachers Pang Xunqin—one of the first artists to paint the minority people of China—and Zhang Guangyu—who illustrated tales from Yunnan Province—reinforced his interest in taking the trip. With the support of Zhang Guangyu he set out for Xishuangbanna in December 1961. The school could not pay for a second student excursion for Ting, so Zhang Guangyu personally financed the six-month journey. Describing the trip later, Ting said,

As I traveled to Yunnan I felt that finally I understood China. This was the first time I had gone from the northern part to the southern part. I went on the slowest train and stopped at every station. It took a long time to get from north to south. When

I got there I felt like I was in another world, very quiet and beautiful. This experience was very important for my art. From this experience I started to find myself. I found my own tranquillity. Previously I had been very excitable and enthusiastic about many things. But now I began to find peace.[37]

Ting Shao Kuang's first impression of Xishuangbanna was that it was not as beautiful as Huang Yongyu had described. Suddenly there were many things he had no means to express in art. For one thing, he was unable to see any color in Xishuangbanna except green, and he could not see the whole, but only individual trees and plants. He sat looking at the scenery for more than a week, not knowing how to paint and not painting anything.

Every leaf had its own shape, every tree had its own character. The color was all the same, but the shapes were different. The foliage was thick and lush; there were so many trees and they were so big. So I just sat and looked at it. Sometimes I would sit in one place for four or five hours without moving and just look. After long, slow observation I began to feel that this foliage was very meaningful. Every tree had its most important point, just as if I were looking at a person and suddenly found the eyes. In the midst of the lushness and confusion I saw the eyes. Then I could paint. I spent half a year just concentrating on the shapes and deepening my paintings, or finding the eyes.[38]

On his return to Beijing six months later in May 1962, Ting Shao Kuang told Zhang Guangyu about his experience discovering the "eye" or the soul of each plant. His teacher was so happy that he embraced him. He took down his own paintings and covered the walls of his small apartment room with the ink paintings of Xishuangbanna that Ting had brought back to Beijing.[39] Zhang's reaction to Ting's thesis work typifies the quality of encouragement Ting received from this most important mentor. Ting's self-confidence as an artist can be traced in part to the support he received from Zhang Guangyu.

Ting was so stimulated by the artistic discoveries and the peace of mind he had found in Xishuangbanna that he was reluctant to return to Beijing. He stayed away from the CAAC, "painting from life" longer than students were ordinarily allowed, which caused some con-

sternation at the academy.[40] When he returned he had completed most of the work required for graduation, and spent the remainder of the summer on his graduation piece, a colorful illustration of a long poem of the Dai people. The work is now lost. At the time, conservative faculty members at the CAAC found contemporary Western elements in it so objectionable that they tried to prevent Ting's graduation. For one thing, Ting included figures that from one angle looked like females but from another angle looked as if they were males. His approach, inspired by modern European art, deviated altogether from the revolutionary romanticism and realism that students were supposed to learn at the academy. While his subject was correct—a celebration of minority life—his style included abstraction and distortion, making it completely out of place in the early 1960s in China.

Three professors bravely stood up for Ting Shao Kuang in the ensuing fracas over his "inappropriate" graduation piece. Zhang Ding, Zhang Guangyu, and the newly-appointed painting department head Yuan Yunfu each gave Ting a 5+ mark—highest honors—overriding the negative votes cast by other faculty members, and Ting was allowed to graduate in August, 1962.[41] In fact, Ting Shao Kuang's timing was fortunate on two counts. One, there was less pressure on artists to conform than there was during the Anti-Rightist Campaign and the peasant-painting movement of the late 1950s; and two, there was even a small concession at the government level that technical training and an appreciation of beauty were important in art if they were combined with correct political ideas.[42] This was a relatively lenient climate for artists between the repression of the previous years and the terrible persecutions that were yet to come. Ting received excellent artistic training, and his graduation piece, though controversial, was accepted. Zhang Ding's prestigious position as leader at the CAAC and his support for Ting Shao Kuang were probably the most important factors in Ting's graduation.

After graduation, Zhang Ding wished to keep Ting Shao Kuang in Beijing to help him with a folk-art project.[43] But Ting himself wanted to return to Xishuangbanna and applied for work in Yunnan Province instead. At graduation he and the other students were given the chance to list six locations in which they would like to work. Ting wrote "Xishuangbanna" on all six lines. There was little competition for work in such a remote area of the country, so Ting was assigned as a professor of art at the Yunnan Art Institute (*Yunnan Yishu Xueyuan*) in Kunming.

CHAPTER TWO
KUNMING AND THE CULTURAL REVOLUTION (1962–76)

AT THE TIME TING SHAO KUANG finished school, most graduates of the art academies in Beijing hoped to stay in the capital. The number of positions in Beijing was limited, however, and many of the artists were sent elsewhere to work. Ting Shao Kuang's voluntary exile from the capital is an indication of his free spirit and his love of beauty. He was eager to return to Xishuangbanna, hoping to join the simple life of the native people there and continue to paint the landscape. The Chinese saying, *tiangao huangdiyuan* ("heaven is high above and the emperor is far away"), seemed to him an apt expression of his situation. People in ancient China used the phrase to describe the freer atmosphere in parts distant from the capital where the watchful eye of government was less intense. Always an individualist and nonconformist in his ideas about art, Ting had no desire to remain in the city among other artists. He felt that he would be able to paint what he liked if he were farther from the source of political control. Although he had hoped to return directly to Xishuangbanna, because of its proximity to the Burmese border he was assigned instead to Kunming. This was a significant disappointment for Ting because he had fallen in love with a young Dai woman while in Xishuangbanna and had hoped to be reunited with her. When he was finally allowed to travel to Xishuangbanna several years after his transfer to Kunming, the girl had married and aged quickly through heavy work and childbearing. A number of his later works are inspired by the memory of this girl of the tropics who had treated him kindly during his stay there as a student.

At the Yunnan Art Institute Ting taught a variety of subjects, including drawing, oil painting, woodcut, Chinese ink painting, Chinese heavy color painting (*zhongcai*), and art history. The artist He Deguang (b. 1945) was a second-year student at the institute's affiliated high school when Ting arrived. He remembers that Ting was different from the other teachers because of his skill as a painter and because of his unconventional ideas about art:

> I immediately felt that Ting Shao Kuang was special. It wasn't just that he was a good painter, but he had different ideas. At that time I didn't really understand modern art. Chinese education was very conservative, and I hadn't heard much about modern art. The art education that we received came from the Soviet Union, and we learned their methods. I didn't really understand Ting Shao Kuang's ideas when he first came either, but I felt that his ideas were not the same as other teachers. When Ting Shao Kuang came he stirred things up in our school and made it more lively. His approach to art was so different from the dogmatism of our other professors. So even though he was very young he influenced many students. We all loved to be around him.[44]

That year there were 80 students at the institute and its high school. Both the high school and college students shared the same dormitory and enrolled in the same classes with little distinction made between them. As an unmarried instructor, Ting lived within the same complex as the students in the dormitory for single faculty members. He Deguang and other students would sometimes seek him out after class to listen to his ideas about modernizing Chinese art. He Deguang recalls:

> He had many theories! When he would talk about his theories he would sometimes severely criticize our works. He didn't like the methods we were being taught in school. I wasn't upset by his criticism, but I was a little afraid of him! He was severe, but what he said was right. He wasn't like the other teachers who wouldn't tell us how we could improve. He would directly tell us which aspects of our work were lacking. He told the truth.[45]

From 1962 until 1965 Ting taught his students at the art institute what he had learned privately from his teachers in Beijing about modern European masters, something he never would have been able to do in Beijing or other large cities. He was often criticized by the conservative school officials, but chose largely to ignore their ire. When he was required to show them his own paintings he produced the standard socialist-realist style paintings, skillfully executed, with revolutionary subject matter, and the officials were somewhat mollified. Ting became good friends with his students; this ultimately saved him from prison in 1967, when one of them warned him of the authorities' intentions and enabled him to escape arrest.

In 1964 and 1965 Ting Shao Kuang was joined in Yunnan by several other young artists who were also to play a part in modernizing Chinese painting:

HE NENG (b.1942) was assigned to teach painting at the Yunnan Art Institute after his graduation from the Sichuan Academy of Fine Arts (*Sichuan Meishu Xueyuan*) in Chongqing in 1965. A native of Sichuan, he had witnessed the starvation death of his own father during the famine that wracked China in the early 1960s. At the time of his graduation the campaign to send graduates to remote places to gain experience had begun. Many of the students of the Sichuan Academy were assigned to work in Xinjiang and Tibet. He Neng had had ten classmates from Yunnan and had been attracted by what he had heard of the colorful minorities and the tropical scenery of the southwest from them. He volunteered to go to Yunnan.

LIU SHAOHUI (b.1940) came to Kunming from the Central Academy of Arts and Crafts to work at the Yunnan People's Publishing House.

YAO ZHONGHUA (b.1939) had been a student with Ting Shao Kuang at the affiliated high school of the Central Academy and then had studied under Dong Xiwen at the CAFA. His student paintings were heavily criticized, and Dong Xiwen was unable to protect him from the harsh punishment of heavy labor in the countryside. In 1964 Yao was sent to remote Kunming and assigned what was considered a lowly position, illustrator for film advertisements.

ZHOU LING (b.1941) had attended the Central Institute of National Minorities (*Zhongyang Minzu Xueyuan*) where Ting's boyhood friend Liu Bingjiang taught. In 1964, during a school-sponsored propaganda project in Sichuan Province, she fell in love with Liu Bingjiang and they were married, violating the institution's strict rules against romantic relationships among faculty members and students. As though they were being punished for the marriage, on graduation Zhou Ling was denied work in Beijing where her husband lived. She knew of Ting Shao Kuang through her husband, admired his work, and decided that, if she could not stay in Beijing, perhaps Kunming would be a more suitable environment than some of the other places of "exile." Liu Bingjiang took some comfort in the solace that his friend would be near at hand if his wife were in need. In fact, Ting Shao Kuang himself returned to Beijing and made the long and hazardous journey, partly by oxcart, back to Kunming with Zhou Ling. Zhou Ling remembers one morning before dawn when Ting Shao Kuang had not yet awoken and the oxcart was ready to leave. Not knowing where in the dark hostel he was sleeping, she let out a terrified scream that woke him (and presumably any other travelers at the hostel) and he hurried to catch up.[46]

JIANG TIEFENG (b.1938) went to Kunming from the CAFA where he had studied woodblock printing and heavy color painting under Huang Yongyu from 1959 until 1964. Because he was considered to have come from a bad family, he was given a menial job in the Kunming Enamel Factory, despite his artistic talent.[47]

WANG JINGYUAN (b.1940), another graduate of the CAFA, went to work at the Mass Culture Center in Kunming in 1964.

In this way a core of outstanding painters began to form in the distant province of Yunnan. Their friendship and exchange of ideas became the basis for an innovative and influential art movement that originated in the southwest and spread as far as Europe and the United States. But first the artists endured the fiery crucible of the Cultural Revolution.

Just prior to the Cultural Revolution, teams of university teachers, including Ting Shao Kuang, were sent to the countryside around Kunming to help a delegation from Beijing carry out what was known as the Four Cleanups (*siqing*). The mission of the Four Cleanups movement as Ting remembers it was an effort to help those in the countryside discover who had mistreated the people and caused the suffering of recent years.[48] Both the peasants and the members of the delegation liked Ting very much because he worked diligently and with good humor. Reflecting later on the experience, Ting said, "I hated the corrupt local officials who mistreated the peasants so I did this work willingly and worked very hard. Whenever I discovered a problem I wrote about it, and it had the effect of the dismissal or arrest of the corrupt official. So the people were very happy."[49] Because Ting was from Beijing, and they had no idea about his family background, the peasants thought Ting must surely be very powerful, probably even more powerful than the Party Secretary of the County. They were awed by this reputed power, and even more impressed by his honesty. Ting Shao Kuang attributes the fact that he was not sentenced to years of hard labor during the Cultural Revolution to the good work he did among the peasants at this time. But like all other intellectuals, he too received his share of trouble and humiliation.

The Cultural Revolution began in the summer of 1966. That same year the Yunnan Art Institute merged with Kunming Normal University (*Kunming Shifan Daxue*).[50] Dance was eliminated, but the music and art areas became departments within the university. Ting Shao Kuang was transferred to the art department at the university along with other members of the art institute faculty, but when the Revolution began all teaching ceased. Classes did not resume until 1970. Because of Ting's family background he was a primary target for the revolutionaries. His progressive ideas and interest in Western art made his situation even worse. Big character posters denouncing him were placed on the walls of the university almost immediately, and he was forced to attend struggle sessions and confess his crimes as a counterrevolutionary. From the summer of 1966 until late in 1967, for nearly a year and a half, he was forbidden to paint. Creating his own works was, of course, out of the question, but he was not even considered worthy of working on the propaganda art that occupied some of the other artists in Kunming. It became difficult for him to meet with his friends, and for about six months he avoided all contacts for fear of causing them trouble. Once while riding a cart in the streets of Kunming he was attacked by a mob of angry Red Guards shouting, "Down with the stinking Counter-Revolutionary Ting Shao Kuang!" The cart driver, undoubtedly to save himself from criticism, pretended that he was so disgusted by the polluting of his cart that he refused to accept payment for the ride.

Every day there were meetings at the school to criticize the teachers and encourage them to write self-criticisms. Ting Shao Kuang was the only professor from the art department to be classified as one of the "four bad elements" (sileifenzi),[51] and his attendance at the meetings was mandatory. He was also assigned to perform manual labor repairing roads in Kunming. "Every morning and evening we counter-revolutionaries had to stand in front of Mao's portrait, bow and repent of our mistakes," recalls Ting. "But when I stood there I cursed under my breath; I did not confess."[52]

When Ting's situation worsened in the summer of 1967, some of his friends and students warned him of his impending arrest and helped him escape from Kunming. First he donned the red armband of a Red Guard and took a train to Tianshui in Gansu Province.[53] From there he walked to the ancient Buddhist cave temples at Maijishan and sought refuge with an old caretaker and his daughter at a nearby temple his friends had told him about. Arriving at the locked compound after dark, Ting pounded on the door, but there was no response. Finally he climbed an old cypress tree near the wall and jumped down into the courtyard where the startled old man was waiting, fearful that the loud knocks had come from Red Guards bent on destroying the temple. Offering the caretaker a bottle of maotai liquor, Ting soon convinced him to let him stay. The daughter brought out two steamed buns mixed with sand that Ting, in his extreme hunger, relished as though they were delicacies given by a bodhisattva.[54] During the days that followed, Ting immersed himself in the beauty of the sculptures and paintings at Maijishan, accompanied by the old scholar who had spent a lifetime researching the works. On the first day the old man carried the little red book of Mao's quotations and asked Ting to read a few quotations while they viewed the art. After both of them had uttered the requisite expressions of distaste for the feudal past, they gazed together on the beautiful treasures of ancient China. On the second day, the book of quotations was left at home and they reveled in the art without formalities. Ting stayed at Maijishan for a month, forgetting the chaos that enveloped his country while he remained in that peaceful enclave. Finally he tearfully left the old man and his daughter, taking with him vivid memories of colorful wall paintings and finely crafted sculptures that would inspire his later works.

From Maijishan Ting Shao Kuang walked back to Tianshui and took a series of trains further west into Gansu Province to an ancient Buddhist outpost along the Silk Road, Dunhuang. As a student in Beijing, Ting had seen an exhibit of copies of the mural paintings from the Mogao Caves near Dunhuang. Now he was free to explore the caves themselves. Here his admiration for the ancient art treasures of China grew even more, and he absorbed a stock of wonderful motifs that would resurface in his own art many years later. Recalling the experience, he said:

> I saw with my eyes that the paintings of Maijishan and Dunhuang were actually very modern. I felt that I was looking at paintings by Roualt—the heavy black lines. The feeling was really modern. I forgot about the tumult and chaos outside and immersed myself in the ancient art.[55]

Ting stayed away from Kunming for six months, and during that time bravely journeyed to Beijing. Although he knew it was dangerous, he went to see each of his former teachers in turn, to pay his respects and to let them know that there was at least one student who had not turned against them. Zhang Guangyu had already died, but he visited Pang Xunqin, Zhang Ding, Zhu Danian (b.1915) and Yuan Yunfu, all of whom were in political trouble. If he could not visit them in their homes, he went to the Academy to see them and bowed to them there. Although he was bodily removed from the school, the work teams and Red Guards in charge at the CAAC had no jurisdiction over outsiders, so he was not harmed. When he was called to a struggle session to criticize Zhang Ding, he refused to say anything more than that Zhang Ding was a good teacher. After two weeks he left Beijing in anger and frustration. Later Ting was repeatedly asked to write confessions about his relationship with Zhang Ding, but he consistently refused to mention any of his teachers in his self-criticisms.

Zhang Ding, who had formerly held a responsible position in the art world, was particularly singled out for criticism during the Cultural Revolution, and his treatment was very harsh. He was forced to work in the boiler room and clean toilets at the school where he had once been leader. At the school he was made to wear a placard and attend "meetings of a thousand people" (qianren dahui) where he was criticized for "learning from tradition" (xiang chuantong xuexi). As part of his torment he was often beaten and even pushed off high platforms where he knelt during struggle sessions; his family and friends worried that he wouldn't survive the physical abuse. Later he was sent to the countryside to do back-breaking work on a military farm. He labored for ten years before he was rehabilitated and returned to teaching at the Academy. His son, imprisoned for more than eight years during the Cultural Revolution, was physically abused to the point that his survival was deemed miraculous. Because of the intense struggle sessions that were held against him at his own school, when Zhang Ding stepped through the door of the school ten years later he nearly collapsed.[56] The physical and psychological strain was more than he could bear for quite some time after.

During the Cultural Revolution, the Red Guards expended their anger on all intellectuals, especially those with foreign contacts and those in high positions, but they singled out Zhang Ding's folklore projects for the most vitriolic attacks. He had collected and studied Water-Land paintings (shuiluhua), works used in Buddhist mortuary rites that included depictions of gods, ancestors, nature spirits, and creatures from each of the Six Realms of Existence. Most of the paintings in his collection had been purchased in common marketplaces. Ironically, these paintings fall easily into the category of popular art, or in Maoist terms "art for the masses," made by anonymous artists for China's general populace. But Zhang Ding's irrational critics held the view that his "direction was wrong" because he tried to "learn from tradition."

In 1966 the school held a black painting exhibition for Zhang Ding so that all could see and criticize his works for their failure to promote the revolution. A second black painting exhibition was held later that was widely publicized and attended by hundreds of Red Guards who were in Beijing from other parts of the country. Guides were posted at the exhibit to explain that the artist was antisocialist and counterrevolutionary. A painting of a cock was pointed out as anti-Maoist—Kruschev had once called Mao Zedong a "fighting cock;" the painting thus revealed that the artist agreed with Kruschev. Another painting, a still-life of a piece of Yangshao pottery, was criticized because someone said the pot was used to hold cremation ashes, symbolizing that the artist wished the revolution would die. Zhang Ding now laughs at the absurdity of the accusations, but at the time one group of Red Guards who heard these interpretations became very angry, demanding, "Where is the guy who painted these?" All the faculty members were locked in the same room like cattle, sleeping on the floor. The Red Guards kicked the door open and called Zhang Ding's name, then dragged him to the basketball court where they forced him to kneel. There a girl from Guangzhou removed her belt and beat him fiercely while the others poured down a rain of insults. "This was only a small-scale struggle session," said Zhang Ding years later.[57]

In Beijing, Ting Shao Kuang was shocked to see that his former teacher's hair had turned completely white. Zhang Ding told Ting that it had turned from black to white in just one night. Ting's visit occurred at a point when Zhang was temporarily released from the school, and he went to Zhang Ding's home for a sparse evening meal of rice. Zhang Ding did not sit at the table, but sadly squatted on the floor to eat his rice in a humble position. Ting squatted down with him and called him "teacher" all the same.

Towards the end of the Cultural Revolution Zhang Ding began to paint in secrecy. Finally, in 1978 he held an exhibition in Beijing to restore his reputation as an artist. Ting then arranged for the paintings to be exhibited in Kunming, once again proving his loyalty to his old teacher. Zhang Ding's daughter, who traveled to Kunming with the paintings, returned to Beijing and reported to her father all that Ting had done for him.[58]

Ting's former classmate Liu Bingjiang suffered a different sort of privation during the Cultural Revolution: he was separated from his wife, Zhou Ling, just ten days after their marriage. His repeated attempts to give up his coveted Beijing residence card and join his wife in Kunming were rejected each time by his school. Zhou Ling was allowed 12 days per year to visit her husband, but during the chaos of the Cultural Revolution she sometimes stayed longer; she gave birth to their daughter in Beijing during one visit in December 1968. Liu Bingjiang taught no classes between 1964 and 1973. Instead he was assigned to do manual labor for that period, including two years of farm work planting fields, tending pigs, and shearing sheep in Hubei. Zhou Ling was unable to care for their small daughter in Kunming, so the baby remained in Beijing with Liu Bingjiang's mother. Liu remembers Hubei Province as being unbearably hot and felt the time there was endless. Finally he returned to Beijing, and in the following year, in 1973, after years of negotiation, Zhou Ling was given a position at the Central Institute of Minorities and joined her husband and daughter in Beijing. Their daughter, Liu Ye, began to paint and proved to be a child prodigy.[59] Though her talent was remarkable, she was never awarded any of the school prizes for art, which went only to the children who painted revolutionary subjects. The Cultural Revolution had not ended, but Liu Bingjiang encouraged his daughter in her art in hopes that a better day would come for her. Even though he felt that his own life had been hard and wasted, he knew the Cultural Revolution could not last forever; it wounded people too deeply, trampling both the truth and people's rights.

In 1968 the fury of the Red Guards began to turn away from intellectuals and focus on top-ranking Communist Party members. Ting Shao Kuang returned safely to Kunming and his job at the Yunnan Normal University where he was assigned some propaganda work, including political cartoons, Mao portraits, and history paintings such as Mao Goes to Anyuan. Since 1966 he had become increasingly dispirited, wondering how he would ever progress artistically. At one low point he noticed that when he looked at reproductions of Michelangelo he felt nothing. Realizing that this boded ill for his own art, he resolved to begin painting again. Working secretly at night he feverishly made drawings based on plaster casts of

Michelangelo's works at the university until his feeling returned. After that he continued to work at night, studying modern Western painters and ancient Chinese motifs, experimenting with ways to use them in his own art. Each day before dawn he would burn the previous night's work so that it could not be used as evidence against him.

In 1968 the Red Guards split into two factions that battled each other senselessly for power in every town across China. The purpose ostensibly was to prove which group was loyal to Mao and which was actually counter-revolutionary, but anarchy reigned, and ordinary citizens were terrified. The fights began with fists and knives and progressed to guns and even the confiscated cannons and tanks of the military. Many young people died in the furor, as often from their own carelessness and inexperience with weapons as from enemy attacks. The school where Ting worked was deserted except for two or three faculty members. Ting volunteered to stay and take care of the library and the music department's record room. Alone at the school he pored over books and listened to recordings of Western classical music day after day for nearly three months while the sounds of artillery raged outside. The bamboo columns of the school buildings were riddled with bullets, but Ting remembers the dangerous time as a period of personal peace and growth. He systematically listened to all the school's recordings—first Beethoven, then Mozart, then others. As he listened he felt his artistic sensibilities returning along with his powerful self-confidence. He continued to paint at night, working to keep his skill vibrant and his soul alive.

One of Ting's contemporaries in Kunming, Yao Zhonghua, remembers that it snowed during the fighting, a most unusual occurrence. Anxious to draw a snow scene, he went to Green Lake Park only to discover that the two factions were in battle there. Undeterred, he hid between two stones so the bullets would not hit him and continued to sketch. Finally the fighting ceased and both factions were required to turn in all weapons. Yao Zhonghua rode along in the truck with others from his factory into the countryside to the arsenal where they were to turn in the arms. Inspired by the beautiful countryside scenery, he quietly dismounted the truck, allowing his fellow workers to continue to the arsenal, and sat by the roadside sketching until the truck came by again on its way back into town.[60] These anecdotes underline the extraordinary will of Ting Shao Kuang, Yao Zhonghua, and other artists like them to use every opportunity to work on their art. While it would have been safer to abandon their painting, they overcame enormous obstacles to keep it alive. Yao Zhonghua, whose father had received a doctorate of medicine from Johns Hopkins University, was under constant surveillance during the Cultural Revolution. His house was ransacked four times by roving bands of Red Guards. Like Ting, he came from a "bad family," and suffered the consequences for many years. Thus the risks these two artists took to make even a little artistic progress were compounded.

When the factional fighting ended, Ting Shao Kuang was appointed the head of the revolutionary committee for the fine arts department at the university, but his appointment lasted only three weeks. He was fired by the Work Team (gongxuandui), the peasants and workers who were in charge of running the school during the Cultural Revolution. Explaining the reason he was let go Ting Shao Kuang said:

> Do you know why I was fired? Because when I called the morning meeting I would very quickly go through the preliminaries, read one article that took twenty minutes, ask for questions (there were no questions), then dismiss everyone. My meetings were too quick and simple! I also liberated a lot of the teachers who had had problems. I would just say, "It seems there is no problem here," and let them go. So I did some good for the teachers at a time when they were having trouble with everybody else. But the Work Team really hated that. I did some good while I had power, but they didn't like it.[61]

In July 1969 Ting Shao Kuang married Zhang Daxi (b.1945). The romantic story of how they met is known by all Ting's friends and extended family. When Zhang Daxi's teacher at the Sichuan Conservatory of Music in Chengdu visited her husband, another professor at the Yunnan Normal University, she saw a painting by Ting Shao Kuang that she thought must surely be a portrait of her student. In fact, Ting had never met Zhang Daxi, but he was intrigued by the idea that his painting resembled an actual woman. He found a way to get to Chengdu so that he could meet the beautiful girl he had dreamed up for a painting, and Zhang Daxi's teacher acted as a go-between.

Since there were no students to teach at the university, Ting stayed several weeks in the conservatory dormitory to court Daxi. When she graduated and returned home to Chongqing, he obtained her address and appeared at her house in Chongqing the next day. Surprised by his boldness, Daxi introduced him to her parents. Her mother, though skeptical because of Ting's bad family background, had an even deeper fear—that her daughter would marry someone who would beat her. She watched for signs that would reassure her of her daughter's physical safety as Ting's wife and eventually was persuaded. To win Daxi's father's consent, Ting painted an enormous portrait of Chairman Mao for the family's home, painting freestyle rather than from the grids that the many hack artists used to churn out portraits of "The Great Helmsman." When Daxi's father saw this he was convinced that Ting had a "golden rice bowl," and would never lack a means of supporting his daugther. Besides, he was also won over by Ting's sincerity and sense of humor. Zhang Daxi's paternal grandmother, who also had a say in the matter, was impressed by Ting's respectful manner. As for Daxi herself, she consented to the marriage because she felt that Ting truly loved her. Neighbors and teachers were surprised she should choose him—she was young, very pretty and from a family with a good political background, while Ting's political status was shaky. But Ting's self-confidence and ardent pursuit helped him win the wife he desired at a time when many others with bad political backgrounds had difficulty finding a mate.

The couple was married, and Daxi returned with Ting to Kunming for a short period before reporting to her assigned job in Dukou, Sichuan. Only those who came from politically correct backgrounds could work in Dukou, and Ting had little chance of finding a job there. However, Daxi was able to transfer to the remote and rustic Kunming without too much trouble, and she soon joined her husband there. She was assigned to sing and play piano with the Kunming Song and Dance Troupe and often traveled with them to the small towns around Kunming, performing revolutionary songs and dances for peasants and workers. Daxi gave birth to a daughter, Ding Ting, on December 11, 1970. Six years later, on April 23, 1976, just a few months before Mao Zedong's death and the official end of the Cultural Revolution, her son, Ding Li, was born.

In 1970 the universities that had been closed reopened, but with a very different type of student body. Applicants were no longer screened for intellectual ability but were admitted on the basis of class background. Those deemed worthy of higher education were soldiers, workers, and peasants. After four years Ting Shao Kuang was a teacher again, and he adapted to the new educational climate with good humor and cleverness so that he became a popular teacher among these politically correct youth as well **(Fig. 12)**. Ting had to be much more circumspect in his instruction of these students. For one thing, they lacked the foundation for art studies that previous students had had and were thus unable to understand many of the concepts Ting had taught his former students. But even if they had been technically prepared, introducing foreign artists like Matisse and Picasso would have been even more dangerous than it had been prior to the Cultural Revolution. So Ting taught academic realism and traditional Chinese painting to these students and continued his own experiments with modernism privately at night, burning the evidence as before. He would later introduce a select few students to modern European art, but for the most part he kept it to himself.

Ting took seriously his responsibilities to these undereducated youths and sincerely desired to teach them the basics of painting. He wanted to teach them figure drawing but knew the plaster models of European sculpture that his former students had used for drawing practice would be condemned as bourgeois by those who knew anything about them. So he hit upon the ingenious plan of introducing the sculptures to the school's Work Team as virtuous revolutionary figures and Chinese folk heroes. Taking the Work Team leaders to the storeroom where the plaster casts were housed, he invented a title for each cast: Head of the Revolutionary Committee, Foreign Lei Feng,[62] or one of a series of comical, nonsensical Chinese names. When Ting came to a figure of Jesus Christ he told them that this was a very good man who taught the masses. The peasants of the Work Team had no idea what the figures were or where they came from, but impressed by Ting's titles and explanations, they approved most of the casts for study. One especially funny anecdote concerns the nude statues:

> When we came to Venus she had no clothes. The Work Team said that Venus and Michelangelo's David were female and male hooligans, so I agreed that they would cause problems and we would not use them. The students were listening outside. One of them said about Venus, "Well, if you don't like her, I'll take her. I think it's very good." With that he grabbed the statue and started to take it away but they chased after him and retrieved it. It was hilarious.[63]

Because of Ting's resourcefulness, the Yunnan Normal University was probably the first art department of the Cultural Revolution whose students were able to draw from plaster casts. Most of his colleagues laughed riotously over the names Ting gave the figures. But one, Lian Weiyun, chastised him: "Ting, I thought you were a cultured, educated man, but now I think you are not cultured at all. Why did you do such a silly thing? It's stupid to give those ridiculous names to the sculptures." Ting replied, "It would be stupid not to do this. If I hadn't, the students would have nothing to draw."[64]

Each year at the Canton Trade Exposition in Guangzhou, Jiang Qing, wife of Mao Zedong and dictator of the arts in China, introduced six new heroes to the Chinese people. An art exhibition featuring paintings of the heroes was also held. In 1970 Ting Shao Kuang was commissioned to paint one of these heroes, a barefoot doctor named Qin Weng. Qin Weng was a minority woman, a native of Zhongdian in Yunnan Province, who traveled to Tibet where she patiently practiced medicine, walking from one village to the next to help alleviate the suffering of the ill and diseased. Ting Shao Kuang painted three large gouache paintings of Qin Weng, each about 60 by 80 inches, and took them to Guangzhou himself.[65]

Ting was also commissioned to choose a girl from Qin Weng's home town to accompany him to Guangzhou and introduce Qin Weng at the trade fair. The girl was supposed to wear the native costume of Zhongdian and relate the story of Qin Weng. To complete his mission, Ting first traveled to Zhongdian, where he found a bevy of girls waiting in a large courtyard, all vying for the position. From a balcony he quickly chose one he liked. She was pretty, but her clothes were old, and she smelled of goat butter. The journey made her nervous; she clung to Ting, calling him "Elder Brother." In Guangzhou, a town known for disliking outsiders and giving short shrift to Mandarin (as opposed to Cantonese) speakers, the girl was snubbed constantly and Ting ended up fighting just to get places in hotels and restaurants for her.

While Ting was in Guangzhou an earthquake struck Kunming, killing four teachers from the university. Ting used the earthquake as an excuse to avoid a meeting with Jiang Qing, who had admired his paintings and requested an audience. There were, of course, many advantages to meeting with Madame Mao, but Ting disliked her and was not interested in tainted prestige. He knew that many others there ardently wished to meet Jiang Qing and the Iranian princess who accompanied her and suspected that his abrupt departure would not cause serious repercussions.

During the next few years, Ting painted more than a hundred propaganda paintings. Though he was interested in neither the assigned subject matter nor the style of social realism, he was thankful to be working. "I was happy to be able to paint, even if it was just Mao's face," he said. "It was far better than having them yell at me and fight with me."[66] When annual national art exhibitions resumed in Beijing in 1970, Ting participated frequently as a representative from Yunnan province, submitting politically safe subjects in keeping with the prevailing winds, while privately continuing to explore a different direction for art at night.

As early as 1969, Ting Shao Kuang's home became a center for passionate evening discussions on the meaning of art and the direction art should take in modern China. Friends would drop by once a week or, by 1972, almost nightly to talk with Ting about the differences between Western and Chinese art and how the two approaches to art could inspire a new art for China. During the dark days of severe repression, the talented young artists who had been exiled to Kunming just prior to the Cultural Revolution sustained each other with their talk. Ting took the lead in these discussions, which sometimes lasted until after midnight, much to the dismay of his wife who was unable to sleep in the tiny one-room shack where they lived.[67] Members of the earliest group included Zhou Ling, He Neng, He Deguang, Yao Zhonghua, Wang Jingyuan, Wang Ruizhang, Lang Sen and occasionally Jiang Tiefeng. If one of them was in some kind of political trouble, he or she would avoid the meetings temporarily. The artists met secretly but talked openly among themselves. "Those of us

who got together to talk were all good friends," Zhou Ling remembers, "so we didn't worry about anyone finding out. We would have gotten in trouble for talking about modern art and Western methods if anyone had known about it. But we knew no one there would tell, so we weren't afraid."[68] Zhou Ling and others recall that Ting was their spiritual leader (jingshen lingxiu). Zhou Ling said:

> At the time I knew Ting Shao Kuang in Yunnan it was impossible for us to paint. So we would get together and talk about art. Ting led the discussions and kept our spirits going. Everyone loved to go to his house and listen to him talk. He encouraged everybody. He was very familiar with modern Western art, so his thoughts were progressive. He took the lead in ideas. His style didn't influence us, but his thoughts really did.[69]

In 1973 two new young artists, Zhong Shuheng (b.1946) and Liu Jude (b.1947), were assigned to work in Kunming, and they joined the spirited evening discussions. Both were recent graduates of the reopened Central Academy of Arts and Crafts in Beijing. They were self-taught artists for the most part, as schooling during those years was comprised more of classes in political thought than anything else. Zhong Shuheng and Liu Jude had not had the chance to "paint from life" that earlier CAAC students had had, so they were enthusiastic about working in Yunnan Province. Ting Shao Kuang's teachers at the CAAC provided them with introductions, and encouraged them to get to know their former prodigy. Although they had been educated at a prestigious art school in the capital city of China, Zhong and Liu knew nothing of modern Western art. Ting introduced them to the exciting discoveries of European art he had made more than ten years earlier in the Beijing Library and taught them the theories about Chinese folk art and ancient Western art history that he had learned from Zhang Guangyu. Liu Jude remembers that other artists in Kunming called Ting the "black flame" because his black hair stood straight up on his head and his face was illuminated almost as if by a light that shone while he talked.[70] Zhong Shuheng said:

> During the Cultural Revolution Ting Shao Kuang really had ways to survive. He was humorous and intelligent. He got along well with the peasants, workers and soldiers who were in charge of the intellectuals. The workers, soldiers and peasants were uneducated and could not understand artists, so the conflicts were numerous. But since Ting Shao Kuang never took them very seriously they thought he was very smart. There were many incidents. I can't remember them all, but Ting really knew how to handle them. He was different, not like the other intellectuals who worried too much. He was not depressed like the others.[71]

The combination of Ting's flexibility and the relatively relaxed atmosphere of the tropics probably allowed for better communication between the artist and his superiors than many of his contemporaries experienced. Once, after a series of forthright discussions with city officials about various problems in the art community, the officials asked artists in Kunming to prove their loyalty by doing a series of paintings on the theme "Down with Deng Xiaoping." Ting, He Neng, and Jiang Tiefeng collaborated on a woodblock print entitled *The Oriole Is Singing* and the *Swallow Is Dancing* (*ying ge yan wu*), which is an adaptation of a Chinese phrase for a fine spring day, and thus conveyed the meaning "everything is going well." In this way they avoided direct criticism of Deng Xiaoping yet still showed what could be interpreted as support of the government's decision to oust him.

Ting not only influenced the artists who lived and worked in Kunming during the Cultural Revolution, but also hosted many of the artists who traveled to Yunnan Province from other cities in China, including Huang Yongyu, Wu Guanzhong, and Zhu Danian. As the Cultural Revolution drew to a close, more and more artists visited the tropical southwest, stopping at Ting's house to join in the lively artistic discussions that took place there. When students from the art academies in Beijing, Sichuan, and Hangzhou began to travel again, Ting also hosted them. Thus dozens of artists eventually fell under his charismatic spell and exchanged ideas about art with him as they

traveled through Kunming. By the time the Cultural Revolution finally ended, Ting and his artist friends in Kunming were fully prepared to set their ideas in motion, and in a very short time burst upon the Chinese art scene with their bold and novel approaches to color, line, and the use of ancient decorative motifs.

While the Cultural Revolution was undeniably a setback for every serious artist in China, Ting Shao Kuang has been able to identify some aspects of artistic growth that would not have taken place under other circumstances. In one way, the secrecy he was forced to maintain for many years was beneficial; it allowed him to paint privately whatever he wanted. Without pressure from others he was able to experiment endlessly, and he learned a great deal. Since he knew from the outset that his works would never be viewed, he painted for no one but himself. His ceaseless copying of Michelangelo's sculpture made him a master draughtsman, a talent he may not have had the patience or time to develop in a more commercial or academic setting. In another sphere, the ingenuity he employed as he coped with poverty, political turmoil, and the great range of people he encountered increased his confidence in his own ability to survive. Unusually buoyant, he sustained both himself and his friends in a time of great trouble. Though the years were hard, they too had a role in forming the man and his art. Paradoxically, the pain of the Cultural Revolution gave rise to the beautiful dreamworlds that Ting Shao Kuang paints today.

CHAPTER THREE
SHEN SHE (1976–1980)

TUCKED AWAY IN KUNMING, having weathered the worst parts of the Cultural Revolution, Ting Shao Kuang and his circle of artist friends continued their nightly animated discussions on art. The initial group grew to include Dong Xihan, Wang Ruizhang, Lang Sen, Dai Guangwen, a teacher at Yunnan Art Institute, and Liu Jude and Zhong Shuheng who arrived from Beijing in 1973.[72] Zhou Ling left the group in 1973, finally able to join her husband, Liu Bingjiang, and their daughter in Beijing. The friends encouraged each other with their dreams of a better day for art in China. Ting was especially optimistic and predicted that in ten years individual artists would be allowed to exhibit once again.[73] The others listened in disbelief, but in fact it was less than ten years before the dream came true. Artistically, the most significant members of the group were Ting, Zhou Ling, who continued to have contact with the group after her move to Beijing, Liu Shaohui, who joined after 1976, and Jiang Tiefeng.

Isolated from the rest of Chinese art society, the Kunming artists did not realize how unique they really were. But in 1975, when a delegation from Kunming visited artists at the academies in Guizhou and Chongqing, they discovered in conversations with their hosts that in fact their own ideas were iconoclastic in comparison. The other artists were still mired in the discipline of academic realism, while the Kunming artists had plunged far ahead in their use of more expressionistic styles. Their goal was to create a new, modern Chinese painting, and their talk was all about how to do it. Gradually, the desire to form a society to disseminate their ideas began to take hold of a few of the leaders in the Kunming art circle. The death of Mao Zedong in September 1976 and the arrest of the Gang of Four the following month gave the artists additional encouragement, though they still proceeded with caution. About the period between 1976 and 1979 Ting said:

That period of time was especially important in terms of our thinking. After Mao died and after the Gang of Four was apprehended, everyone was ecstatic. China started to have hope again. At that time we started to talk about forming an art organization. But at the time I think we were working not for strength in art but for political strength. We were fighting against censorship of our art.[74]

After Mao's death and the arrest of his wife and her cohorts, the artists meeting at Ting's house became less secretive and the numbers grew. All the young painters who had been banished to Kunming in 1964 and 1965 attended. Stories of the lively atmosphere of these meetings abound. According to Luo Wenzhi and Tong Jingxia, the wives of artists He Neng and He Deguang, Ting would stand on a table in the tiny room of his house to deliver his energetic speeches. A kettle of boiled water was continuously on the stove, and individuals took turns serving water to the others. Sometimes, because of the large numbers, the group would meet at Yao Zhonghua's house, which was bigger. Tong Jingxia said:

There were no opportunities for exhibits or meetings. The only way they could exchange ideas was to meet privately in each other's homes. In Ting's tiny house there was only one table for painting and no chairs. Almost every night and on Sundays or holidays many people went to his house—colleagues, friends, and admirers. They talked about art. Ting could really talk! He always gave lectures. Everyone loved to hear him and would sit and listen.[75]

Ting's magnetic personality and love of teaching drew others to him. As the first of approximately twenty young artists to move from Beijing to Kunming in the early 1960s he naturally assumed a leadership role. But it was his knowledge, his artistic passion, his generosity, and his fearless optimism that gave him the charismatic power that reinforced his position as leader.

Shen She Is Organized

As early as 1964 Ting had dreamed of forming a circle of artists in Kunming and had even made plans for it with Yao Zhonghua. At the time they were young and full of hope, but the Cultural Revolution set them back fifteen years. Finally, in 1979 Ting and Yao and a core group of close friends formally organized an art society called Shen She. The government had recently relaxed restrictions on artistic creation and had proclaimed a second period of "let a hundred flowers bloom," indicating that differing styles and approaches in art would be tolerated. Not completely trusting the current official policy, the artists planned their organization carefully. According to Ting:

It was still a little bit dangerous at the time. So we said we can't have the responsibility for this organization on just one person's shoulders. All five of

*us must head this organization. If we choose a
leader he will be the scapegoat in case of trouble.
We must all share the responsibility.*[76]

Thus the standing committee responsible for the organization of the society consisted of Ting, Yao Zhonghua, Liu Shaohui, Wang Jingyuan, and Jiang Tiefeng. He Neng, Wang Ruizhang and Jia Guozhong were to serve as secretaries.

The name *Shen She*, or Shen Society, has several layers of symbolic meaning. The coming year, 1980, was the *geng-shen* year according to the Chinese cyclical calendar. As the first year of a new decade, 1980 symbolized a time period during which the artists fervently hoped they would have opportunities to express themselves in a freer artistic climate. Translated as "1980 Society," the name Shen She signals a time to begin anew and leave the deprivation and humiliation of the Cultural Revolution to the past. The coming year was also to be the "Year of the Monkey" according to the lunar calendar. By referring to 1980 in the name of the group, the Shen She members alluded to all the meanings that the monkey has in China in their title. In the preface to their 1980 exhibition catalog, they wrote that the "Golden Monkey" stands for truth, loyalty, wisdom, courage, and the people's ideals. These were fine words for a printed document in socialist China and were meant to legitimize the formation of a private group. What remained unspoken, but certainly in the thoughts of every member of the group, was the audacious and rebellious side of Monkey's character as portrayed in the novel *Journey to the West*. As noted in Chapter One, Ting's teacher, Zhang Guangyu, had used illustrations of Monkey's adventures to satirize the corruption of Guomindang officials in the 1930s. Ting and the other leaders of Shen She could just as easily have pointed the same satirical finger at abuses by Communist officials thirty and forty years later. More important to them, however, was the invincible, iconoclastic nature of Monkey's character. Just as Monkey broke through the conventions of a dictatorial and bureaucratic heaven, Shen She also hoped to bring something fresh and real to the stultified academic art world in China.

In addition to the symbolism of a new beginning that 1980 conveyed, and a breakthrough in the art world that the Year of the Monkey stood for, the word *shen* had other significant meanings that fit the artists' situation very well.[77] *Shenming* means to set forth, explain or expound. Ting had spent years privately sharing his ideas about art. He and his friends were anxious to "set forth and explain" the many theories that they had formulated during their evening discussions. Thus another translation of Shen She is "Illumination Society." Another meaning of the word *shen* is "to appeal," such as to appeal for justice. *Shenbian* means to defend oneself, *shengao* means to file a complaint at a court of law, and *shenyuan* means to appeal for

justice regarding a false charge. This reference to righting the many wrongs the artists had suffered during past years was also not mentioned in the exhibition brochure, but surely gave the name Shen She even stronger symbolic significance to its members. One other interesting meaning of *shen* is its reference to the time of day. *Shendan* means from night till morning, and *shenshi* means from 2:00-4:00 A.M. Night was the only possible time of freedom for the artists during the Cultural Revolution, the time when Ting Shao Kuang painted and held the discussions with friends that eventually led to the formation of Shen She—the Night Society, the Appeal for Justice Society, the Illumination Society, the New Decade Society, the Society of the Year of the Monkey.

Purpose and Ideals of Shen She

Many of the goals of Shen She are implicit in the name chosen for the society by its leaders. According to Yao Zhonghua, their purpose was twofold: to unite the talented artists of Yunnan and to form a movement of modern art in China. Yao said, "The ideas were already there in 1964, but because of the Cultural Revolution could not move forward. During the years of the Cultural Revolution the artists matured, and emerged with new energy and more people to create a new style of painting."[78]

While the emphasis was on the modernization of Chinese painting, one did not have to conform to a specific style in order to join Shen She. One of the main criteria for membership, however, was that one's paintings not be political. Ting said:

Shen She became a strong organization, and the twenty or more members were ones that we chose ourselves. We didn't want just anybody in it. If an artist were political rather than devoted to art we didn't want him. In order to join an artist didn't necessarily have to paint modern art, just what he liked. So of the twenty or more people in Shen She we certainly were not all of one approach. Most members had their own artistic point of view, but the one thing we had in common was the desire to exhibit freely without having to cater to the requirements of a government-sponsored show, but to paint exactly what we wished. Each of us sought individual artistic freedom. We paid no attention to a person's political background, but focused on personal artistic merit.[79]

He Neng also emphasized that freedom from political constraints on art was one of the primary goals of Shen She:

The goals of Shen She were very simple: to get rid of the shackles that bound artists and let them express themselves freely without censorship from the government. Since the Communists took over they've had the idea of controlling the artistic process. Artists were always perceived as being tools for the revolution and they weren't allowed to create freely. So artists have been oppressed for a long time. In the beginning a lot of artists accepted those conditions of restraint. But it became increasingly intolerable. The oppression of the Gang of Four was what really became intolerable. As the pressure became more intense, the more artists rebelled. Before the Gang of Four was crushed, the first sign of the repression becoming intolerable was the demonstration in Tiananmen Square after Zhou Enlai's death. After the demise of the Gang of Four in October 1976 it seemed, at least on the surface, that there was hope for China. There was a temporary relaxation for the masses, and at the same time the artists felt a sense of freedom. Shen She was formed under those conditions. Everyone was trying to find freedom, creativity, the intrinsic worth of artistic creation. One of the main reasons for Shen She was to have greater freedom. The other main point of organizing Shen She was to throw off political influence in our art.[80]

After fifteen years of painting works to promote socialism in China even as they endured untold suffering for imaginary crimes against the state, it is no wonder that Ting and his artist friends sought to divorce their works from politics. But to believe they could safely do so was surely naive. Not long after the organization of Shen She, and even before its introductory exhibition in July 1980, an official backlash against the "Hundred Flowers" freedom in the arts was brewing. A speech by official art spokesperson Zhou Yang, head of the China Federation of Literary and Art Circles, published in December 1979 reminded writers and artists that politics and art were inseparable:

Literature and art are reflections of social life; they exert a tremendous influence on life....
Fundamentally speaking, the relation between literature and art and politics is one between literature and art and the people. Our literature and art should reflect the life of the people, their needs and interests in the different periods of revolution.... As long as literature and art truthfully reflect the people's needs and interests, they must exercise enormous influence on politics. To talk about breaking away from politics can only lead our literature and art astray.[81]

Before repressive measures took effect, however, Shen She members successfully held a major exhibit made up of pieces that made little attempt to be politically correct. Because of the success of this exhibit, the Shen She

artists felt that they had reached their goals as an organization. They had gained national recognition and had all exhibited freely—just once, but that one time fulfilled the dreams of many years.

The Exhibition in Kunming

Twenty-three artists exhibited 120 paintings and prints at the Yunnan Museum in Kunming in July 1980 under the title: "Shen She: First Exhibition". Although the exhibition was officially sponsored by the Yunnan Branch of the Chinese Artists' Association, there was no required subject matter or set agenda for the exhibition. Ting Shao Kuang left China on the eve of the exhibition, leaving only one small ink painting for the show **(Fig. 13)**. Miraculously, he had heard from his sister and mother in the United States, and he acted immediately, securing a visa on the pretext that his mother was ill and he must travel quickly to see her. His timing was right, and in a series of unusually lucky events he was able to exit the country. Yao Zhonghua took responsibility for collecting the paintings for the exhibition, and from that point took over Ting's leadership role in Shen She. But Ting remained "honorary president" of the group until its dissolution in 1982.

The twenty-three artists included three women, Li Xiu, Liao Yin, and Chen Zhichuan. There were three minority artists: the woman Li Xiu, who was from the Yi minority group; Ke De'en, who was a member of the Man tribe; and Dong Xihan, who was Bai. There was also one married couple—Chen Zhichuan and Zhu Weiming. The other artists were Ting Shao Kuang, Wang Tianren, Wang Jingyuan, Wang Ruizhang, Liu Shaohui, Sun Jingbo, He Neng, He Deguang, Meng Xueguang, Li Kaiming, Lang Sen, Xiao Jiahe, Yuan Ruixin, Yao Zhonghua, Jia Guozhong, Pei Wenkun, and Jiang Tiefeng **(Fig. 14)**.

The exhibit was accompanied by a brochure of a quality that had not been seen since before the Cultural Revolution, beautifully printed at the factory where He Deguang worked. He Deguang carefully watched over the printing process of the small production, and its high quality graphic design is a source of pride for him to this day. "Shen She: First Exhibition" is printed boldly on the cover in black and gold characters on an orange-red and black background. On the reverse cover is a monkey design, both mischievous and decorative in black, orange-red and gold **(Fig. 15)**. Inside the front cover is a calligraphic inscription by Wu Zuoren (b.1908), the former president of the CAFA, made for the group when he visited Kunming. The favorite disciple of Xu Beihong, who worked with Xu to establish socialist-realist art in China, Wu Zuoren was an odd choice for the inscription. Yet he was impressed with the works of these Kunming artists, and his prestige lent credibility to the exhibition.

The preface to the exhibition states:

In order to create a new visual world which is characterized by a clear revolutionary spirit, by its own people, and by its own time, and in order to create the truth, goodness and beauty of minority art, we have banded together to form this painting organization, Shen She.

Shen She was born in the Year of the Monkey, which is the first year of the 1980s, the calendric geng-shen year. The golden monkey is the incarnation of one who seeks truth, loyalty, wisdom, courage, and liveliness, the incarnation of the ideals of the people. We have used him as the symbol of Shen She. On the complicated and arduous road of art, only those who possess his spirit and character can undertake the heavy responsibility that history has bestowed on our generation.

We are fully aware that without a theoretical breakthrough there will be no new creations in practice. Without free experimentation and brave exploration and practice, everything is empty words. The basic characteristic of art is creativity. Without creativity, art will die. The character of the painter himself is the essence of style, thus the basis of painting is to forge one's own spirit. Thus we desire to study, ponder, discuss, and practice.

The works exhibited at this time are mostly the experimental pieces of the members of Shen She, done for practice. They are only the beginning of the first step. But we hope that one day we can exhibit the true fruits of our diligent labor. Then we will present it to the people and to history, who are the judges of what is selfless and great in truth and in art.[82]

Despite the political rhetoric and the self-effacing tone of the preface, the paintings and prints that were shown in the exhibit were truly innovative in comparison to the works that had been done in China during the previous two decades. Though the exhibition was held in remote Kunming, it caught the attention of the art world in Beijing and other parts of the country. Yao Zhonghua compared the effect of the exhibition to throwing a stone into a pool of water. "The ripples upset the smooth water."[83] The exhibition was favorably reviewed in the art journal of the CAFA, *Meishu yanjiu*, in Beijing in January 1981, and reproductions of paintings by five of the artists were printed.[84] In May 1981, the Shanghai art journal *Meishu congkan* printed articles by Liu Shaohui and Jiang Tiefeng along with fourteen color and twenty-six black-and-white reproductions of works from the show.[85]

The *Meishu Yanjiu* reviewer, Zhou Liangpei, praised the Kunming artists for using new compositions, colors, line, and light to "depict the reality of our society." The

writer criticized China's former closed-door policy that prevented artists from learning about new styles and techniques and referred to the Shen She artists as part of the new "thinking generation." Works based on the modern European masters that Ting had admired so much and discussed enthusiastically with his students and friends were finally acceptable. The irony is that the acceptability was still couched in political language. To depict the "reality of China's society" was one of the dictums of Zhou Yang's speech about the close relationship between politics and literature, and the "thinking generation" was the new catchword for those who had previously been duped by the Gang of Four during the Cultural Revolution but would not be led astray again. It is also ironic that by the time Chinese artists began to explore the revolutionary European artists of the early twentieth century, American artists had already taken art far beyond cubism into pure abstraction and back again. What was fresh and modern to Chinese eyes was pleasing, but not surprising, to Westerners.

The exhibition included woodblock prints, lithographs, drawings, works in gouache, gouache and ink paintings (also called *zhongcai* or heavy color painting, the distinctive medium that later became the feature of "Yunnan school" painters), oil paintings, and traditional Chinese paintings. The majority of the works were figures, but there were also landscapes, still lifes, and a few flower paintings, such as the highly original but somewhat melancholy cluster of wildflowers by Dong Xihan **(Fig. 16)**. A number of the artists made the minority people—their stories, festivals, and daily life—the subjects of their works for the exhibition. He Deguang painted a hauntingly beautiful scene of Dai girls supplicating Buddha early in the morning of the traditional water-splashing festival **(Fig. 17)**. Minority figures were a politically safe subject, but religion was not. The obvious piety of the women is pleasingly portrayed, and the viewer is left with a feeling of profound respect for the religious beliefs of the people. These two paintings alone demonstrate the changed climate for artistic freedom. Not five years earlier Dong Xihan's work, a painting with no message other than to show the beauty of the night flowers, would have been called dreary and depressing, an attempt to dim the glorious light of the revolution. The portrayal of religious faith by He Deguang would also have been condemned, and his dark colors criticized. Socialist-realist paintings showed happy people working in the full light of the sun, not superstitiously praying before dawn.

Repose by Sun Jingbo **(Fig. 18)** is a loving picture of a minority woman suckling her child in an attitude of complete rest and enjoyment of the moment. Though she carries a heavy load and is seated in a rocky landscape, it is her resting that is emphasized rather than the work she must do. Compared to the many depictions of vigorous workers—in fields, factories, and mines—during the previous thirty years, this close-up view of repose is refreshing.

Jiang Tiefeng drew on a legend of the Sani people to paint *Ashima* **(Fig. 20)**. Because Ashima refused to submit in marriage to a wicked man, she was trapped by water he sent rushing through a ravine and drowned. The beautiful girl turned to stone, and when the water receded her stone likeness remained. Visitors to Shilin (The Stone Forest), near Kunming, still listen as Ashima calls out to her brother who bravely tried to save her. Jiang portrayed the violent moment of Ashima's death in the whirlpool with a combined energy and gracefulness. The distorted figure of the girl stretches across a wild, abstract pattern of whirling water and the flattened shapes of doves. The birds hold white flowers in their mouths, an offering for her burial.

The woman stretched out across a Chinese opera mask in Chen Zhichuan's *June Snow* **(Fig. 19)** is reminiscent of Jiang Tiefeng's *Ashima*. She seems to be another innocent sacrifice to the designs of evil men, the eyes of the giant mask glaring coldly behind her. The colorful swirls of the mask are inspired by traditional designs for the theater. Chen explores the color and shape of the stage art and twists them into abstract patterns against which she places the figure of the girl. The girl's scarves trace the curves of her body and echo the movement of apsaras, the flying attendants of Amitabha Buddha as they are depicted in the Dunhuang cave murals. The title of the painting is possibly a reference to the story, "June Frost," published in the China Women's Journal (*Zhongguo nü bao*) in 1908, shortly after the execution of the feminist political activist, Qiu Jin. Snow or frost in June is an unnatural event, just as the execution of a young woman and the persecutions of the Cultural Revolution were unnatural. Though the Shen She exhibit was praised for showing the "reality of the life of the people," it was never intended by the government that abstract expressions of suffering and a twisted world be included in the depiction of reality. Generic scenes of daily life were what was prescribed. It is a stretch of the imagination to include Chen Zhichuan and Jiang Tiefeng's works in this category—another indication that the Shen She artists took their quest for artistic freedom in socialist China to the outer limits of acceptability and were still successful.

Pei Wenkun did show the "reality of the life of the people" in a remarkably fresh and innovative way. Painting from a bird's-eye view, he looks down on the patterns of ordinary life and raises them to the realm of art. A cluster of bicyclists is reduced to simple geometric shapes and the repetition of a few basic colors against a gray ground **(Fig. 21)**. The pleasant bustle of a morning ride to work is conveyed with great economy. *Clear Day* **(Fig. 22)** is another example of Pei's skill in economy of means. The cheerful feeling of a fine, sunny day is simply conveyed through a bird's-eye view of colorful pieces of laundry drying in the

yard of a traditional Chinese house. The only part of the house that shows is the corrugated rooftop on three of the sides that form the courtyard. He Neng also shows a glimpse of daily life in *Day Off* **(Fig. 23)**. A young girl relaxes with a book at her very ordinary, gray plaster-over-brick window. There is no attempt to show that she is productive or reading anything of political note. The birds beneath the window sill are common sparrows. There is no revolutionary glory in her posture or face. Both Pei Wenkun and He Neng convey the pleasant ordinariness of life without preaching.

One painting from the exhibit, *Golden River* by He Deguang **(Fig. 24)**, depicts two women bathing, one of whom is nude from the waist. The painting is clearly based on French impressionist models. Shimmering water surrounds the bathers who are caught in an unconscious pose, a fleeting moment. In China during the 1920s the propriety of paintings of nudes was a serious question for artists interested in drawing the human figure. Liu Haisu in Shanghai was the first to introduce the use of nude models in the classroom in 1926, and he encountered strong opposition from the local government. After 1949, under the new socialist regime, paintings of nudes were completely out of order and were rarely made, even in private. This tentative reintroduction of nudes in a public exhibition was actually quite daring and is another indication of the freedom that Shen She artists reached out to embrace with the hope that it was really there. While some paintings of nudes were tolerated, others caused disproportionate problems for the artists who made them, suggesting that politics was still more important than art. The case of some highly objectionable nude bathers painted as part of an airport mural by Yuan Yunsheng, an artist influenced by the Kunming circle, will be discussed in Chapter Four.

One of the eight paintings shown by Yao Zhonghua in the exhibit was an expressionistic rendition of the *qi* or "spiritual essence" of a bull **(Fig. 25)**. The bull stands defiantly on high ground, a dark silhouette against a display of turbulent colors. The vibrant motion of the sky behind the bull suggests upheaval, perhaps symbolic of both the violent past and the revolutionary growth that was taking place among Shen She artists.

Most of the Shen She artists discarded the romantic realism that had been patronized since the founding of the People's Republic in 1949. Liu Shaohui is the one who moved closest to abstraction in his works *The Lute Player* **(Fig. 26)** and *The Tai Household*. The dark, rich colors and heavy black lines of both paintings were inspired by the French painter Rouault. Ting Shao Kuang had noticed the affinity between Rouault and Dunhuang figure paintings of the Northern Wei period when he visited Dunhuang in 1967, and he enthusiastically introduced Rouault to his circle of artist friends. *The Lute Player* shows a couple caught up in the swirling melody of the lute played by the man.

The melody envelops them in an embrace that is both tender and disturbing, holding them together yet surrounding them with turbulent sound. The houses in *The Tai Household* are dissolved in geometric shapes and patterns of color, forming an abstract design that suggests a neighborhood. Ultimately, however, it is the shapes and colors that are the real subject of the work.

The work left by Ting Shao Kuang for the exhibition recreates the serenity of an actual river in Xishuangbanna, the *Liushahe*, or "Flowing Sand River." It is one of twenty-nine minutely-detailed sketches that Ting made in preparation for the mural project in Beijing that he completed just prior to his departure from China. Liusha River was the last recognizable landmark in China for Monkey and the other pilgrims journeying to India in Wu Chengen's *Journey to the West*, the place where "Sandy" joined the group. The gracefully protective tree and the wide expanse of placid water, the relaxed minority figures and the peaceful cranes make no reference to the events of the novel whose hero the Shen She artists admired. But surely it is no accident that Ting chose this piece from among the sketches he had recently finished. Liusha River was the point of departure into the unknown for Monkey. High adventure and buddhahood awaited the hero of the novel, and Ting must have wondered what lay ahead in his own future. The painting left behind was a reference to the energetic goals of Shen She, the Year of the Monkey Society, but it was also a personal symbol of Ting's newly won freedom to leave China.

Exhibitions in Beijing and Hong Kong: Shen She Dissolves

Though far from the capital, the remarkable exhibition organized by the Shen She leaders caused a stir in the art world, and the suggestion was made that the exhibit be held again in Beijing. The artists themselves could not afford the expense and approached the Yunnan Provincial Cultural Bureau for funding. Unwilling to support a privately-organized group, the Cultural Bureau agreed to fund six of the Shen She artists along with four other Yunnan artists. In September 1981, the ten Yunnan artists held an exhibition in the Beijing Art Gallery *(Beijing Meishuguan)* that aroused a great deal of curiosity and was well attended. Zhang Shiyan said, "Shen She was one of the most important exhibitions after the Cultural Revolution in Beijing. Many people went to see it. The works were very appealing to those who viewed the exhibit because the artists depicted the beauty of life and society."[86] But He Neng felt that the Beijing exhibition was the government's attempt to water down the radical elements in Shen She and make the show less effective. "There is a Chinese expression, 'add sand to rice,' which makes it inferior," he said. "That's what they did to the Shen She exhibition."[87]

The Shen She artists who exhibited in Beijing—He Neng, Yao Zhonghua, Wang Jingyuan, Liu Shaohui, Jiang Tiefeng, and Jia Guozhong—were the leaders of the group and among the most important artists. The artists that accompanied them from Yunnan were Zhang Jianzhong, Liu Ziming, Li Zhongxiang, and Yao Yongmao. According to He Neng, it was the practice of the Beijing Art Gallery to collect at least one work from each artist who exhibited at the gallery. As a result of the increasingly sensitive political climate, and the controversy sparked by the show in Beijing, the gallery refused to accept the works of He Neng, Liu Shaohui, and Jiang Tiefeng.

A symposium was convened by the official Beijing arts magazine, *Meishu*, to discuss the works in the exhibition from Yunnan. Twenty distinguished artists and critics, including Wu Guanzhong, were invited to attend. A number of other artists, such as Liu Bingjiang, Yuan Yunfu, and Chen Danqing also attended. Although the *Meishu* report of the symposium carefully outlined the ways in which the artists' works fit into current policies for art, in fact the arguments at the symposium about the paintings were heated.[88] It was at this meeting that one of Jiang Tiefeng's works was described as a "nightmare," to which one artist retorted that he would be glad to dream like that every night.[89] One faction at the meetings attacked the works for pursuing the aesthetics of form and color without regard to the message of the painting. In truth, the Shen She artists were interested in "art for art's sake," though that had only been admitted privately among themselves. But none of them was purely formalistic in his approach; in fact, one of the aims of the organization had been to focus on life and its beauty. Wu Guanzhong spoke eloquently in favor of the pursuit of beauty in art, and Liu Bingjiang, Yuan Yunfu, and others also defended the Yunnan painters. In the end the artists were not punished, but some of them were discouraged. They felt that the contributions they had to make were not appreciated in China. Ting Shao Kuang encouraged them to join him in the United States, and during the next few years many of them did.

Despite the lack of freedom the artists felt after the ten-person show in Beijing, the strong response among artists in Beijing to the exhibition was a measure of the innovative approaches to art of the Yunnan painters. The article about their works in *Meishu*, though carefully phrased, was positive overall in its praise of the exhibition. Even the abstraction in Jiang Tiefeng's paintings was defended: even though he used abstract forms his art could still be understood by the people. The article noted that the beauty of the works in the show attracted people, even without the endorsement of political leaders, and concluded that the Yunnan painters had provided a new aesthetic experience.[90] The painting chosen for the journal's cover, however, was not one of the modernists' paintings, but a traditional Chinese landscape by Wang Jingyuan.

The following spring, a few of the Shen She artists' paintings were shown in Hong Kong at the First Institute of Art and Design, along with Ting Shao Kuang's works. Liu Bingjiang and Zhou Ling, then living in Beijing, were invited to join the show as well. Most of the works in the show were done in the traditional Chinese technique of heavy colors on Korean *gaoli* paper that was revived in the twentieth century by Huang Yongyu and Yuan Yunfu, and were inspired by Yunnan scenery, Yunnan minorities, and the Dunhuang mural paintings. The exhibit was a great success in Hong Kong and widely covered by the press. It was through this publicity that the term "Yunnan School" came to describe the artists who used the heavy color technique.

After the successful Hong Kong show a second Shen She exhibit was planned in Kunming in 1982. Several artists had already left Kunming for Beijing, Hong Kong, and the United States, but Yao Zhonghua began to collect works from those who stayed behind. Another conservative wind blew through China in 1982, however. Yao was summoned by an official from the provincial Cultural Bureau and advised to both disband Shen She and cancel the exhibition. Under pressure from the government, and lacking the enthusiasm and leadership of Ting Shao Kuang, Shen She ceased to exist. Despite its short life, the artists were satisfied that they had reached important goals through the organization. They compared themselves to the Impressionists of the nineteenth century, a group that was also short-lived but that had an incalculable impact on the Western art world. As Yao Zhonghua recounted, "The Shen She group shocked the establishment which for years had painted socialist-realist art and pictures of Mao. They broke through old prejudices, then scattered."[91]

The Yunnan School

While Ting Shao Kuang dreamed about and planned for an art circle like Shen She from the first year he lived in Kunming, the term "Yunnan School" was actually invented by others. The name was used loosely in Beijing in the early 1980s to refer to all artists who came from Yunnan Province. From the journal *Chinese Literature:*

> Twenty years ago a number of young artists settled down [in Yunnan] after their graduation from the Central Academy of Fine Arts and the Central Institute of Applied Arts in Beijing. Recently an exhibition of oil paintings by ten Yunnan artists was held in Beijing, a tribute to their work over the years. It aroused such interest in art circles that these artists have been acclaimed as the "Yunnan School." Though their styles are not alike, the content and form of their paintings is typical of Yunnan.[92]

At the same time in the capitalist countries outside China the term Yunnan School was used to describe a specific style that some of the Kunming artists were using. Ting Shao Kuang had formed a unique combination of Chinese line, Chinese-style heavy colors, motifs from Dunhuang, and the flat, distorted figures of Western painters like Picasso and Matisse in his paintings. Under his influence, a number of other painters in Kunming experimented with the effects of heavy colors combined with modern Western styles. Zhou Ling taught the group what she had learned about heavy color painting from Huang Yongyu, and Ting taught them about ancient Chinese art motifs and modern European masters. The innovative amalgamation of these elements had startled the Chinese art world and caught the attention of the Hong Kong market. The artists who painted in this "modern heavy color" style began to be referred to as the "Yunnan School." The name itself is evocative, calling up images of a faraway tropical land peopled with exotic minorities. The story of the artists who came from there is also romantic—a brave group of painters who held on to their artistic ideals in a remote setting, emerging as true innovators in the Chinese art world after twenty years of seclusion. When the works of these artists began to sell, the name "Yunnan School" was used to promote them. While "Yunnan School" could be used to describe Ting Shao Kuang and his artist friends in Kunming from 1976 to 1980, the name is surely a misnomer now, as very few members of the original circle are left in Yunnan. It is also perhaps premature to call any contemporary group of artists a "school." A more accurate (but less romantic) way to describe the painters would be the Zhongcai Group, or "Modern Heavy Colorists." Currently, hundreds of younger artists are employed by galleries in Hong Kong, Taiwan, and the United States to imitate Ting Shao Kuang's style, and they too are called members of the "Yunnan School." Some of the artists are actually recruited from Kunming, but just as many live outside China and have never been to Yunnan Province.

The Legacy of Shen She

Success and attrition decimated the group that sustained each other with courageous talk during the dark days of the Cultural Revolution. But Ting Shao Kuang left a legacy in China that is both stylistic and theoretical. The unusual talent and energy of the artists who settled in Kunming in the 1960s, guided by Ting's knowledge and leadership skills, made the unlikely little city of Kunming a center of artistic ferment. The banishment to Kunming originally intended as a punishment or demotion for the artists who were sent there actually set the stage for a kind of growth that was unanticipated. The inspiration the artists derived from the tropical scenery and the exotic minority people, the relative freedom they felt in a remote province far from the capital, and Ting's enthusiasm for modern art were all important elements in nurturing an incipient art movement that has affected the entire Chinese art world. The Kunming artists' special inheritance was the courage to seek artistic freedom and a belief in the importance of their own ideas.

The influence of Ting's style can still be seen among the second- and third-generation artists in Kunming. Bold colors, an emphasis on line, distortion of figures, and detailed clothing design are common elements in the works of a number of young Kunming artists.[93] Some of Ting's former students in Kunming are commissioned by art dealers in Taipei and Hong Kong to copy Ting's works, but aside from "business" they work on their own styles, carrying on Ting's search for artistic freedom.

Ting's influence spread far beyond Kunming, however. As mentioned earlier, he was host to all the artists who traveled to Yunnan Province. He also took care of the artists' students. Wu Guanzhong, who became a close friend of Ting through these visits, said:

[Ting] is a generous, passionate person. He always was a friend; he always provided room to stay and materials for the students who went to Yunnan. His painting is just like his person. He was very generous and shared everything he had.[94]

These traveling artists joined his nightly discussion groups and saw his paintings. The exchange of ideas was particularly significant

for the city-weary artists from Beijing. Huang Yongyu, the teacher of Jiang Tiefeng, was an especially welcome visitor. During the Cultural Revolution Ting, Jiang, and He Neng smuggled paper to Huang in Beijing because he was refused supplies. Thus the personal ties between Huang and the Yunnan artists were strong and artistic exchange came naturally. The time spent in Yunnan with Ting was also pivotal in the formation of the art of Yuan Yunsheng and Qin Yuanyue (b.1940). Yuan relied on what he had learned during his stay with Ting for inspiration for the controversial airport mural he created in 1979. Qin adopted the heavy color technique of the Yunnan artists and drew on minority themes to form the graceful style for which he is now well known. His painting *Summer* was shown in the exhibition celebrating the thirtieth anniversary of the founding of the People's Republic of China at the National Art Gallery in Beijing, October 1979. It depicts minority women picking bananas in tropical Yunnan. The elegant, elongated figures are related to the figures in Ting's work.

The Shen She artists who adopted the heavy color style of Ting Shao Kuang are among the most successful today. Ting had an important stylistic influence on Jiang Tiefeng, Liu Shaohui, Zhou Ling, He Neng, and He Deguang. With the exception of Liu Shaohui, who now lives in Guilin, these artists are in the United States, supporting themselves through the sale of their paintings. With his characteristic generosity and loyalty to his friends, it was Ting himself who arranged the exhibitions and invitations to the United States that led to their emigration.

CHAPTER FOUR

THE WALL PAINTING MOVEMENT (1979–1980)

AS **CHINESE ARTISTS** regained their vitality after the Cultural Revolution, government commissions for large public works helped some of them restore lost reputations. Interest once again focused on the revival of wall painting. Enthusiasm for wall painting was generated among Chinese artists searching for a way to modernize Chinese painting in the 1930s and 1940s. Zhang Daqian's ambitious project to copy all the paintings at Dunhuang (1942-44) and the subsequent exhibition of copies in Chengdu, Sichuan, in 1944 stimulated further interest in the medium. After the Communist victory in 1949, Dong Xiwen, one of the major participants in Zhang Daqian's Dunhuang project, taught some *bihua*, or wall painting, classes at the Central Academy of Fine Arts. Ting Shao Kuang's professor, Zhang Ding, established a murals department at the Central Academy of Arts and Crafts in 1959. The artistic appeal of the Dunhuang paintings, a source of nationalistic pride, was the major factor in the attraction they held for contemporary Chinese artists. Their divergence from the stylistic mainstream of literati landscape paintings made them a fresh source of inspiration. Because China's ancient wall paintings were painted by anonymous artisans rather than elite intellectuals, they also fit into a socialist context. Chinese artists were impressed by the mural paintings of the Marxist artists in Mexico as well. That Siquieros, Rivera, and Orozco had so successfully used mural painting to champion the cause of socialism also influenced the movement towards mural art in China. It seemed to Zhang Ding and Dong Xiwen that they had found an exciting format for a modern Chinese art. But during the chaotic years of the 1960s and 70s, it became impossible to establish the new art form. In the late 1970s artists were given another chance to realize their creative potential. Zhang Ding, who had suffered intensely during the Cultural Revolution, was invited to direct the first important project, the decoration of the Beijing airport. From that point, mural painting became a fundamental aspect of modern Chinese painting.

The Beijing Airport Murals

Zhang Ding was approached in 1978 by airport officials and the ministry of culture to select artists to submit sketches for the airport murals. Nearly twenty years earlier he had established a mural painting department at the Central Academy of Fine Arts with the goal of reviving mural painting in China, but his ambition had been thwarted by political movements. Now he was offered the chance to renew his goal and call on other talented artists to assist. As president of the CAFA he was familiar with the decorative abilities of many young artists. He immediately contacted Ting Shao Kuang in Kunming and asked him to come to Beijing to join the project. It seemed politically astute that at least one room include works depicting the national minorities from Yunnan Province and it was generally agreed that Ting Shao Kuang, as the leading artist in Yunnan, should create the paintings for that room. Yuan Yunsheng also submitted designs for the airport murals based on his stay of several months in Yunnan province. In an interesting turn of events, it was Yuan Yunsheng who actually won the commission to paint the mural of the minorities. According to Zhang Ding, Ting gave up the commission so that his good friend Yuan Yunsheng would have the chance to restore his reputation as an artist: Yuan, who had the misfortune of being labeled a Rightist while still a student, had endured a severe and protracted persecution. In a gesture typical of his generous nature, Ting withdrew his sketches and allowed Yuan to take his place, then to save face for his friend, used his mother-in-law's ill health as an excuse to return to Kunming. Ironically, Yuan Yunsheng's completed murals were singled out for criticism because in them he depicted two nude bathers. Yuan became well known because of the problems his work caused, but his paintings were eventually covered so the public could not see them.

The mural painted for the airport by Yuan Yunsheng was called *Water-Sprinkling Festival: In Praise of Life* **(Fig. 27)**. Covering two walls of one of the restaurants, it depicted the colorful new-year celebration of the Dai people of Yunnan Province. Nearly a hundred figures in a jungle setting joyfully engage in the many postures and activities of celebration, especially water splashing. In one corner a group of maidens, two of whom are nude, bathe and wash their hair. It is this small section that sparked the controversy over the appropriateness of Yuan's painting. The playful splashing of water, as well as the hair-washing, recall an ancient Dai story in which the maiden responsible for killing a monster-oppressor washed herself clean of the tyrant's blood. Freedom from oppression and the joyful celebration of life were an especially appropriate metaphor for Yuan, who had returned to Beijing after a seventeen-year exile in the northeast, and for the Chinese people, who rejoiced in the capture of the "monsters"—Jiang Qing and other members of the Gang of Four—blamed for the Cultural Revolution. The theme was politically correct and the painting itself beautifully executed. Yuan had every reason to expect that finally he would be accepted back into the mainstream of artistic activity in China, but in fact, he was disqualified from receiving any more public commissions. No longer able to work within the fluctuating restrictions for art in China, he eventually emigrated to the United States.

The time Yuan spent with Ting Shao Kuang in Yunnan influenced both the subject matter and style Yuan used in *Water-Sprinkling Festival: In Praise of Life.* The jungle trees are modeled on the lush, detailed foliage of Ting's landscapes of Xishuangbanna. The uninhibited simplicity of the Dai people was attractive to both Ting and Yuan, and their conversations centered on methods to depict that unconscious freedom in art. One source of inspiration was the Mexican muralists who had made such a deep impression on Ting as a youth. Rivera and Siquieros were masters at depicting the daily life of the Mexican peasants. Yuan also shared Ting's enthusiasm for modern European art, the wall paintings at Dunhuang, and the use of line. His graceful, elongated figures, like Ting's, are a combination of the two-dimensional figures at Dunhuang and the flat, planar figures of Matisse and Modigliani. Through these stylistic means Yuan painted what he had learned about the tropical paradise introduced to him by Ting. Ting's romantic vision of the gentle beauty of Xishuangbanna and its people was the vision that informed this initial work of Yuan Yunsheng.

Another of the airport muralists, Zhu Danian, also owes the inspiration for his piece to time spent with Ting Shao Kuang in Yunnan province. *Song of the Forest* **(Fig. 28)** is a brilliantly colored depiction of a jungle river in Xishuangbanna. After Zhu designed the work, he and his assistants painted it on three thousand ceramic tiles that were fired at the old imperial porcelain kilns at Jingdezhen in Jiangxi Province.

Five other large murals at the airport received considerable attention: *Nezha Subdues the Dragon King* by Zhang Ding, *The Mountains and Rivers of Sichuan* by Yuan Yunfu, *The Spring of Science* by Xiao Huixiang (b.1933), *Towering Trees* by Zhang Zhongkang, and *The White Snake Legend* by the husband-wife team Li Huaji (b.1931) and Quan Zhenghuan (b.1932).[95] Xiao too had spent time in Yunnan Province and attended the night discussions at Ting's house. Li and Quan had visited Dunhuang and drew motifs directly from what they saw there.

Each of the seven major works completed by these artists for the airport combined stylistic elements from both Eastern and Western art. Chinese folklore, national minorities, and scientific progress, and China's mountains, forests, and rivers comprised the subject matter. These subjects appropriately focused on themes that would appeal to foreign visitors as well as promote nationalistic pride among the Chinese themselves. The artists and their assistants worked feverishly for nine months to finish the murals in time to celebrate the thirtieth anniversary of the founding of the People's Republic in October 1979. The new art form was impressive, and Zhang Ding's career was relaunched. The artists had revived the ancient Chinese tradition of wall painting, yet given it a modern look. Before the project was finished, mural paintings for other public buildings were already under commission, and the mural painting movement had begun.

Xishuangbanna Drawings

Excited by the prospect of the airport commission, Ting set off on a forty-day trip to Xishuangbanna to make drawings for the painting he believed he would do. In March and April of 1979 he walked over 50 kilometers through villages, into the jungle, and along the Liusha River. Wrapping rice paper around his legs for protection against mosquitoes, he stopped to sketch when he came across just the right tree or piece of foliage. He carried paper and a small board with him to sketch on, a little at a time, then rolled the paper up as he went. Ting also used the traditional Chinese method of absorbing nature, memorizing its most impressive visual aspects, then recreating it in imaginative ways later. When he returned to his guesthouse each night he employed traditional Chinese brush techniques to make his compositions. Instead of a regular brush, however, he used bamboo pens he made himself, patterned after the ones made by the Dai people for writing. He also used rich, black ink on smooth, heavy *tongzhi* paper. With an incredible outpouring of artistic energy, Ting completed 29 meticulously detailed works that go far beyond their original purpose as preliminary sketches. The drawings are actually a variant of *baihua*, or colorless paintings, a traditional Chinese medium that emphasizes line alone and requires precise skill. They were published in August 1979 by the Yunnan People's Publishing House with a preface by Wu Guanzhong:

> When I returned from Xishuangbanna to Kunming and saw Comrade Ting Shao Kuang's drawings I felt deeply touched. His painting is powerful and profound. Not only is he skillful in the overall structure, but the details are extremely fine. Although we call it drawing, it incorporates a variety of rich middle tones. It is not a photographic record; the entire composition was carefully and deliberately planned.
>
> I love Ting Shao Kuang's drawings because they give the feel of beauty, they have character, and they can inspire. He does not seek surface prettiness, or flirting with the viewer.

*Bananas and mangoes surround people's homes.
Dense forest and prolific vines grow like wild grass.
The bamboo houses especially inspire the painter.
The young Dai wives are slim and pretty.*

*This poem of mine describing the beauty of
Xishuangbanna is composed of many lines. But
Ting Shao Kuang used only one line. With spear in
hand he caught the feeling of Xishuangbanna. Wu
Guanzhong, May, 1979, in Beijing.*[96]

The album features reproductions of eighteen tropical landscapes, some of them more than ten feet long, and eleven figure paintings of Xishuangbanna minority people in their villages. The paintings themselves are now scattered throughout Asia and the United States, as Ting sold them individually to support himself when he first arrived in California. *Meili, fengfu, shenqi* (*Beauty, Richness and Mystery*, **Fig. 29**) is more than twenty feet long, and was sold in two pieces; one half is now in Japan and the other in the United States. The long horizontal work was inspired in part by Zhang Ziduan's *Qinming shanghetu* of the twelfth century. While the subjects of the two paintings are radically different, Ting admired the meticulous attention to details and the strong sense of place in Zhang's work and tried to capture the same spirit in his detailed account of Xishuangbanna. Like Zhang's painting, one cannot see the entire work at once, but must view it as though walking slowly through the jungle. Along the way are numerous carefully planned sections of strikingly beautiful trees and plants. Each leaf and stem is exquisitely portrayed in minute detail. The spatial balance of each section is perfect. Dark foliage contrasts with light in a rhythmic progression through the landscape. In small pockets of space in the foreground, Dai women pluck and carry jungle fruits, their graceful figures blending with the lines of the trees. A bull with a crane on its back is hidden in the foliage near the center of the painting. A few cranes fly freely near the tops of some of the trees. The cranes and the Dai women do not interact, but this seems to be the introduction of the motif of women and birds that recurs in a large number of Ting's later works. Though rich in detail, the painting is not busy. Each scene is tranquil, and the message conveyed is one of peaceful contentment.

In *Tropical Rain Forest* the tonal contrasts are more subtle and the ink more thickly applied to portray the dense luxuriance of moist botanical growth **(Fig. 30)**. The width of the descriptive line varies from wiry thin to nearly a quarter of an inch thick. The ink is shiny, which adds to the portrayal of rich, wet foliage. The trees grow in dense, tangled masses from the bottom of the long, vertical painting. The center group of trees is especially rich and full, so that the formal balance of the painting is again perfected. The upward progression of the trees, one group growing in profusion on top of another, skillfully conveys the overwhelming abundance of growth in the rain forest. It is evident that Ting is thoroughly familiar with the compositional elements of traditional Chinese painting, but he converts the expected rocks or boulders to trees. Where previous landscape painters built mountains from the bottom up, he used components of tropical plants to move upward through fore-, middle- and background. The only figures in the lush scene are a small group of Dai women who bring fruit to wash in the stream at the very bottom of the painting. The women are small and barely noticeable in the dense forest. Their presence, however, suggests humans at peace in their surroundings. They are separated by more than ten feet from a group of cranes at the top of the painting. Ting's red Chinese seal is in the lower right-hand corner.

Besides numerous landscapes, Ting's album also includes a few drawings of Dai houses nestled in jungle settings. Ting envisions the open houses made of bamboo and thatch as scenes of domestic tranquility. One detail shows women peacefully performing household tasks **(Fig. 31)**. Another portrays a woman with two small children on the veranda of her house **(Fig. 32)**. The setting behind her is a tangled mass of jungle trees. The small figure in the richly textured, protective environment is reminiscent of the scholars placed in mountain hideaways by the fourteenth-century painter, Wang Meng. A woman in a domestic jungle setting, however, is completely contrary to Wang Meng's intent. In his modernization of Chinese painting, Ting has expanded the subject matter to include themes never imagined by the former literati artists.

Drawings of young women from various tribes complete the album. This type of realistic portrait of minority figures was first done by Zhang Guangyu in the 1930s, and remained popular through the decades that followed. Ting's figures all have the same dreamy, faraway look— young people contemplating their own future and hoping it will be fortunate. The faces of the girls resemble the face of his own lovely wife, who sat as his model many nights during the Cultural Revolution. Each figure is drawn in its tribal costume and placed in a carefully planned setting. The Wa girl shoulders a rifle, standing on a rock lookout against a background of bamboo **(Fig. 33)**. The Dai girl sits on a bamboo bench on the veranda of her house with tropical plants all around **(Fig. 35)**. The Hani girl is in an architectural setting, her solid black robes and shadows a contrast to the outlined costumes of the other figures **(Fig. 34)**.

The drawings Ting made in preparation for the airport commission include some of the finest works of his career to this point. The two long landscapes are extraordinary in their formal beauty and in the jungle atmosphere that is captured with ink alone. Ting's tremendous outpouring of creative energy was a result of the immense joy he felt in the commission and in the new artistic freedom afforded artists by the government's "let a hundred flowers bloom" policy. After many years of secretly practicing his craft in hiding, he was given the opportunity to paint something that visitors to China from all parts of the world would see. Ting devoted his heart and his energies fully to the drawings, and they remain fresh and masterful variations on traditional Chinese painting.

The Great Hall of the People

Although Ting did not paint a mural for the airport, the sketches he made while trekking through Xishuangbanna served him well in another important commission, a painting for the Yunnan room in the Great Hall of the People on Tiananmen Square. Each room in the massive building was to be decorated to represent a different province of China. The Chinese Artists Association of Yunnan Province assigned Ting Shao Kuang, Jiang Tiefeng, and Yao Zhonghua the task of making paintings for the Yunnan room. Ting responded with an exquisitely colored representation of the Xishuangbanna forest.

The project, though approved by the Ministry of Culture, was initiated and organized by one of the leaders of the Chinese Artists Association, Hua Junwu (b.1915). The success of Zhang Ding and his band of muralists was a sore point for Hua Junwu, who hoped to achieve his own measure of fame in a game of one-upmanship against Zhang Ding. Many established, politically correct artists were left out when the airport paintings were commissioned; their irritation with the wall painting movement is probably the real source of the criticism of the innocuous nudes in Yuan Yunsheng's painting. At any rate, with Yuan's problems in mind, the artists from Yunnan were instructed that landscapes would be preferable to figures, unless the figures were small and clothed.

Ting began work on the painting for the Great Hall of the People in February 1980. Working at a feverish pace, he completed the piece, which is approximately twelve feet high and thirty feet long, in less than four months. He first made the design, then searched for a space in Kunming large enough in which to execute the painting.[97] Tong Jingxia, wife of his friend He Deguang, arranged for Ting and Jiang Tiefeng to use the dining hall of her workplace, which belonged to the local athletic association. As ground for the painting, Ting mounted silk on rice paper. He carefully outlined each plant and figure of the composition with a deep black ink imported from Germany. Then he reinforced the black with gold to sharpen the effect of the line. Last he used a combination of materials to achieve the brilliant colors and texture of the finished product—Chinese mineral pigment, gouache, acrylic, sand, and glue. He divided the painting into six panels, which were shipped by rail from Kunming to Beijing and placed on the east wall of the Yunnan room.

Ting's mastery of line, so beautifully displayed in the monochrome paintings he did in 1979, is maintained in every detail of the immense painting, which he titled *Meili, shenqi de Xishuangbanna* (*Beautiful, Mysterious Xishuangbanna*) **(Figs. 36-37)**. A thin but vibrant gold line defines a hundred different types of jungle plant. The huge trees dominate the painting, but the tiny, lithe figures in the foreground of the fourth panel—Dai women carrying fruit baskets and water vessels—seem unaware that they are overwhelmed by the foliage. They walk peacefully through the trees, and the scene is infused with tranquility, a tropical paradise. In the right middle ground is a cluster of houses surrounded by a bamboo fence. A small Buddhist pagoda is near the little village. The figures, trees, and houses are set on a forward-tilted plane, so that beyond them, where one would expect the horizon and the sky, is the river. Its water, golden in the sun, contrasts with the deep shadows of the forest floor. A few slender boats, placed horizontally to add to the calmness of the painting, float in the golden water. The exquisitely outlined trees are filled in with sumptuous hues, revealing Ting's complete mastery of color. His use of blue, green, and gold recalls the decorative court paintings of the Tang Dynasty. The rich, reddish-brown of the thatched village roofs, echoed discreetly in just the right number of plants, forms a pleasing contrast with the brilliant blues and greens that dominate the picture. Tree trunks and lower leaves of plants are light in hue, standing out against the dark black forest floor. The upper foliage is darker, placed against the golden river for vivid contrast. As in the paintings of 1979, the balance is perfect. In color, line, detail, and decorative effect, the painting is truly a masterpiece.

Ting traveled to Beijing with the painting in June and oversaw its placement in the Great Hall of the People. Hua Junwu was immensely pleased with the work and prepared to have it publicized throughout China. Its beauty surpassed any of the airport murals, and Ting had managed to depict a subject similar to that of Yuan Yunsheng without including anything that could possibly have been found to be offensive. Hua expected that the attention the airport murals had received would be deflected to the Great Hall of the People, and his project would win admiration in place of Zhang Ding's enterprise. But Ting Shao Kuang left China suddenly on July 1, and Hua Junwu's scheme was foiled. To publicize an artist who had fled China would have been a grave mistake. The Yunnan room was closed to the public, and only a handful of Ting's friends ever saw his work.

The painting Jiang Tiefeng did for the Yunnan room is the same size as Ting's, and he used similar materials, but the style and effect are completely different. Jiang depicted *Shilin, the Stone Forest* near Kunming, the place where Ashima was believed to have drowned and turned to stone **(Fig. 38)**. While Ting's painting is fairly realistic, Jiang's is only a few steps away from total abstraction. The rocks of

Shilin form a dark, crowded background and reflect in the middleground river. A huge banyan tree spreads across the foreground, almost unrecognizable with its tangled mass of strange shapes. The white components of the tree stand out brightly against the blue stones. The base of the tree is made up of designs from Chinese opera masks. Minority girls and boys perform a joyful dance underneath the tree, and beyond them, on the far left, stands a goatherd with his white goats. Scattering cranes fly out of the tree at the right of the picture. The dominant blues and whites contrast with bits of red, gold and black. Because of its high level of abstraction, Hua Junwu was as unwilling to publicize the work of Jiang Tiefeng as that of an artist who had escaped from China.

The third painting in the Yunnan room is Yao Zhonghua's romantic rendition of the Jinsha River **(Fig. 39)**. Sunlight streams down on the panoramic view of rugged mountains and swiftly flowing water. Nationalistic pride in the great beauty of China's landscape is effectively conveyed in this massive work, which is painted in oil on one continuous piece of canvas. Yao, an officer in the Yunnan Cultural Bureau, had cautioned Ting and Jiang in Kunming not to make their paintings too big for the room. But when Ting and Jiang arrived in Beijing they discovered the wall space was actually much larger than the works they had prepared. Ting now laughs about the rivalry, but Jiang was very angry when the paintings were installed. Both Ting and Jiang would have preferred to cover the walls with their paintings, fully joining the wall painting movement that they avidly supported.

After the installation of his painting in the Great Hall of the People, Ting did not return to Kunming. Before leaving Kunming he had obtained a passport with the approval of his school. But the school held onto the emigration papers that Ting's mother and sister had sent from California, believing that without them Ting would be unable to secure a visa. With the help of an officer in the American consulate in Beijing, however, Ting miraculously obtained the visa and left without further delay. He spent two weeks in Hong Kong, then arrived in the United States on July 19, 1980.

Zhou Ling and Liu Bingjiang

Meanwhile, the wall painting movement gained momentum in China. Another project directed by Hua Junwu was the decoration of the Beijing Hotel, a prestigious establishment designed to house foreign dignitaries and visitors to China. One of the members of Ting Shao Kuang's former circle in Yunnan, Zhou Ling, together with her husband, Liu Bingjiang, Ting's friend of many years, received a commission to paint the wall of the ground-floor restaurant in the hotel. The commission came through Huang Yongyu, who introduced them to Hua as artists knowledgeable about China's minorities. Both of them taught at the Central Institute of Nationalities. Zhou Ling had spent eight years in Yunnan Province among China's minority populations. Liu Bingjiang had lived in Xinjiang and studied the minority people there. The subject of the mural, already determined by Hua Junwu and the Beijing Hotel, was to be a depiction of representative figures of all of China's minorities, a mural that would educate foreigners about the cheerful subgroups in China as they dined.

Zhou and Liu began work on the mural in 1980. To utilize the best light, they painted only during the day, and then only when the restaurant was closed—mornings from 10:00 to 11:00 and afternoons from 3:00 to 4:00. First the canvas was stretched over the entire wall, then the outlines of all the figures were drawn. The lines were so precise and beautiful that when Wu Zuoren, president of the Central Academy of Fine Arts, came to inspect the painting, he thought it was already complete. Like Ting, Liu and Zhou believed line was the essence of Chinese figure painting, and they had mastered it well. Next the earthy green and brown colors of harvest were applied in acrylic to the canvas.

The painting, *The Joys of Creation and Harvest* **(Fig. 40)**, shows seventy-seven figures in minority costume rejoicing in the fruits of their labor. The human figures are joined by a hundred different birds and animals, reflecting Zhou Ling's great love for animals. The figures are shown in a variety of activities—dancing, feasting, caring for children, tending flocks, preparing food, harvesting grapes, and courting. In one particularly joyful scene a woman lifts her baby into the air, where birds and flowery circles surround it. The mother next to her tenderly caresses a nursing child, while a little girl leans on her shoulder and a cat curls itself up at her feet. The figures reflect happiness and peace. Vigorous movement and strong emotion are avoided, so that the painting elicits a quiet, joyful response from the viewer.

The figures themselves are flat and decorative, some shown in the profile poses of ancient Egyptian mural art. The figure style was influenced by the flat figures of Matisse, whom Liu and Ting Shao Kuang had admired together as early as the 1950s, as well as by the crowded activity in paintings by the Mexican muralists Siquieros, Rivera and Orazco, and by Liu's direct experiences in copying Dunhuang murals with his teacher Dong Xiwen. Though their style is unique, Zhou and Liu drew upon the same inspiration as Ting had in seeking a new form for modern Chinese art. They combined Chinese line with a Western medium and motifs to achieve something universal, an art that could speak to both worlds. Ting's role as mentor and friend added immeasurably to the monumental outcome of this piece.

When the mural was completed in 1982 it was an instant success and was reproduced and written about in major art journals, a response that Hua Junwu had planned for Ting's painting two years earlier. The Beijing Hotel project achieved a glorious depiction of minorities that overshadowed the problematic mural by Yuan Yunsheng.

Minorities as Subject Matter

Beginning with the airport commission in 1979, the wall painting movement in China became an important means for artists to establish their reputations. The popularity of the medium grew as China opened its doors to foreign travelers and businesses. Hotels and public buildings in every major city became venues for China's muralists. The entire October 1981 issue of *Meishu* was devoted to reproductions of new murals and essays by muralists. Reproductions of the socialist Mexican murals and even some photographs of outdoor murals in New York City were also included.

One of the most popular and successful subjects of the muralists in 1979 and the early 1980s was the minority people of China. The major commissions at the airport, the Great Hall of the People, and the Beijing Hotel were dominated by this theme. Artistically, the costumes and exotic customs of the minority people are attractive to artists. But the predominance of this subject matter in mural painting, and in many other arts, suggests that something more than their colorful ways prompted artists to paint them. During the 1930s the study of minorities was China's response to the worldwide interest in folklore, and it also contained a component of nationalism. For the artists in the 1970s and 80s, minority subjects provided material for fantasy, a chance to escape the political reality of their lives and consider an idealized lifestyle. In much the same way as Europeans regarded the "noble savage" of America, Chinese artists imagined that minority people lived a more peaceful and natural lifestyle than did the politically harrassed Chinese in the cities. To paint them or their habitat was to paint one's own version of a utopian society.

Personal interest in the subject was no doubt augmented by the fact that minorities were a politically safe subject. As long as the minority people were clothed and painted in a recognizable style, there was little fear of recrimination. In many cases it was predetermined that the subjects of the murals would be the national minorities. When China became a socialist country, a great deal of propaganda effort went into creating the image that the minority people living in the border regions of China were pleased to be a part of the new China. In the late 1970s and early 1980s, with sophisticated and skeptical foreigners arriving in China each day, efforts were redoubled to depict happy scenes of the minorities in public art. The "Hundred Flowers" campaign was also broadened to include encouragement of the minority members themselves to participate more actively in the creation of socialist art and literature.[98]

Ting Shao Kuang was first attracted to the subject of minorities through his teacher, Zhang Guangyu, who collected folk art in the 1930s. After his own experiences meeting minority people living in Xishuangbanna, Ting admired their simple and easy-going lifestyle and adopted a vision of these people as dwelling in a tropical utopia that he longed to join. Consistently aloof from politics, he painted the minority people because he found them charming. But his main interest was in the landscape and the houses they inhabited.

In summary, Ting Shao Kuang's involvement in the wall painting movement crowned a long period of secret preparation for an unknown opportunity. His interest in the medium began at the time of Siquieros's visit when Ting was an undergraduate art student in Beijing. Ting's early and varied interactions with artists who became prominent muralists after Mao's death influenced the ideas and even the styles of many of them. His love of the minority people and his experiences in Yunnan Province proved acceptable to established authorities, and gave him the chance to paint the masterpiece of his career, the depiction of the Xishuangbanna forest for the Yunnan room in the Great Hall of the People. Had he remained in China, Ting would have become famous. He chose instead the harder road, preferring freedom to fame.

CHAPTER FIVE

THE COLOR OF SUCCESS (1980–1995)

AFTER ARRIVING IN THE UNITED STATES, Ting Shao Kuang was quickly assimilated into the Chinese community in Los Angeles. Before long his paintings sold well among wealthy Chinese professionals in the Los Angeles area. He held numerous exhibitions in university galleries and in business places such as banks. One of his first successful shows was sponsored in 1981 by the Bunker Hills Art League in Los Angeles, the Foundation for the Advancement of Minority Artists. Through the league he befriended other minority artists, mainly hispanics and blacks, and was stimulated by artistic exchanges with them. Though he was slow to learn English, he had a charismatic way of expressing his artistic ideas that defied language. He taught Chinese brush painting at the University of California at Los Angeles, communicating with his students through the medium of art and body language. By 1984 he was able to purchase a modest home in the United States and bring his wife and two children from China to live with him and his mother.

Not satisfied with local popularity, Ting toyed with the idea of making limited edition prints of his works. He and an attorney friend, Sam Rubino, began to look for a publisher. Rubino sent photographs of Ting's painting to Ron Segal, a publisher of fine art prints. Segal was immediately attracted to Ting's art, and in February 1986, within two weeks of their first meeting, the two signed a contract to work together.

While Segal knew that Ting's art was impressive, he was unprepared for its instantaneous success in the art market. The three introductory pieces he took to a dealer's show in New York sold quickly at high prices. From 1986-1994 Segal published limited edition prints of thirty-nine works by Ting and introduced Ting's paintings and prints to markets in Japan and Paris. The particular style that Ting developed in the United States sold well overseas, making both artist and publisher wealthy in less than four years.

Matching the Medium: Translating Mineral Pigment and Gouache to Silkscreen

In the United States, Ting's subject matter evolved from landscapes and minority figures to idealized figures from a multitude of different cultures and time periods set against gorgeously patterned backgrounds. To paint his figures he uses media that he had experimented with in China and was able to perfect in America. On Korean-made *gaoli* paper he first draws the lines of his paintings in black, gold, and silver. He then adds color with a variety of mediums—gouache, acrylic, and Chinese mineral pigment. To intensify the colors he uses a Chinese technique from the Song dynasty (907–1279), brushing ink or dark Chinese colors on the reverse side of the painting. He uses many layers of colors to paint the luminous skin of his figures, with an effect that is extremely difficult to match in printmaking. Ting has been fortunate, however, to find a master printmaker who is willing to take pains to create fine works that reflect his mastery of color.

Gary Lichtenstein of SOMA Fine Art Press in San Francisco collaborates with Ting to produce technically brilliant reproductions of his paintings. The two artists have worked together since 1986 when Segal approached Lichtenstein with the first painting by Ting he wanted to publish, *Harmony* **(Fig. 67)**. For Lichtenstein that first title has special significance, because he believes it is the close relationship he has developed with Ting that ensures the success of their collaborative effort. He prefers to call the prints he makes interpretations or translations of Ting's paintings rather than reproductions, because he relies not just on his superb technical ability to make prints of Ting's works, but also on the application of a great deal of emotional energy. Lichtenstein spends hours thinking about each color that goes into every print. If certain colors don't match perfectly he is not overly concerned; he is more concerned that each print feels right. Lichtenstein believes that he and Ting see with the same eyes and that they understand each other. When he looks at prints of artists' paintings, he can tell immediately whether or not the printmaker and the painter have a good relationship. Lichtenstein admires Ting, who he believes truly understands the give and take of energy and who "lovingly gives energy."[99] Though they faced language barriers at the beginning of their relationship, they understood one another as artists, communicating through the common language of "color, light, forms, and textures."[100]

Lichtenstein and the technicians he employs at Soma Fine Art Press spend two to three months creating each print. The colors are planned by Lichtenstein in consultation with Ting. Then under Lichtenstein's direction the artist Tetsumi Minoh paints the images with hand-mixed colors on at least thirty, and sometimes as many as forty-six, acetate screens. Often it takes ten to fifteen colors for the skin tones alone. The thirty or forty colors combine in different ways to produce a multitude of hues that capture the essence of Ting's original works. Each screen is checked for color and texture, then carefully registered on the press. As each successive layer is added to the print, the work is evaluated. At a certain stage in the life of every print Ting is consulted again to discuss its progress. When the work feels right to both artists, editions of 450 or 500 prints, some on cotton rag paper and some on hand-made rice paper, are individually printed. Then Ting makes another visit to the print shop to sign the finished prints.

Dreams of a Better World: Recurring Themes in Ting Shao Kuang's Art

"My art doesn't reflect my current life," admits Ting Shao Kuang. "I paint what I remember from books, stories, movies, and experiences with other cultures." His friend in Beijing, Zhong Shuheng, stated, "He never took politics seriously. I really think his success in the United States is partly because of this character trait."[101] Ting draws on many rich sources for the subject matter for his painting. He believes the ancient Chinese maxim that one must "walk ten thousand miles and read ten thousand books" before one is qualified to paint. His love of literature, his curiosity about other cultures, and his knowledge of world art history all provide inspiration for his work. While his themes do not reflect the events of his life, they do reflect all that he loves. His art is deeply influenced by the life he has led.

One subject that Ting avoids is the pain he experienced during so many phases of his life in China—the loss of his mother as a young boy, the misunderstanding of his curiosity about Western art as a student, the repression and recrimination of the Cultural Revolution that he suffered as a professor. "I keep the pain to myself," he concedes, "and give only what is beautiful to others." In China he painted scenes of tropical paradise, tranquil settings for exotic but gentle people. In the United States his subject matter has broadened, but the underlying theme of every painting is still beauty and tranquility. The depiction of a dreamworld has been the traditional approach to subject matter taken by literati painters in China for hundreds of years. Despite the turmoil Chinese people have experienced during the entire twentieth century, little of contemporary Chinese art expresses their anguish. In his devotion to quiet beauty, Ting thus continues a Chinese artistic tradition. But it is perhaps also his own personal way of coping with the difficulties he has experienced.

The most pervasive themes in Ting's art are: mother and child, exotic places, Chinese myths and stories, hunting, wind and water, music, dreams, and utopian landscapes. These themes are romantically based, and related to each other. The mother and child motif, evident even in the village scenes of Xishuangbanna made in 1979,

encompasses his profound respect for the bond between women and their children. His infatuation with this subject is no doubt influenced by the thirty-year separation from his own mother, and the emotions caused by the eventual reunion with her in the United States. Paintings of distant lands and ancient tales also stem from his romantic imagination. They reflect Ting's enjoyment of literature and his voracious appetite for reading, as well as his insatiable curiosity. Through hunting themes Ting explores his affinity for animals and his aversion to killing them, and fantasizes about the ambivalence ancient hunters might have faced. Depictions of wind and water express his lifelong fascination with rivers and the sea, the navigation of which can lead to lands unknown. Musical themes relate not only to his love of Western and Chinese music, but also to his idea that the lines in a painting should flow like a melody. The many dreams depicted in his art reveal his identification with people who hope for a better future, especially young girls who are traditionally the ones most often at the mercy of others' will. Many of his paintings express an obvious delight in women and strong empathy for their concerns.

Mother and Child

Ting has made more than twenty depictions of women with children since coming to the United States. Unlike traditional depictions of children in Chinese art, most of the little ones are girls. The women either hold the children or rock them to sleep. *Cradle Song* **(Fig. 41)** was inspired by an Indonesian song called "Bao Bier," translated into Chinese and made popular in the 1960s, that Ting liked very much when he lived in China. The lyrics tell how the mother disguises her fears for her husband at war and sings a reassuring lullaby to her daughter, promising her that her father will return. Ting set the scene in Xishuangbanna because one of his students in Yunnan gave him the song on a record accompanied by a transcription of the lyrics. Behind the mother and child are beautifully outlined palm fronds and other tropical plants similar to those found in his paintings of Xishuangbanna in China. The figures and plants are set against a dark, textured ground that indicates night. The long back and neck of the mother form one side of a wide triangle that anchors the figures securely in their setting and provides a formal balance suggesting peace and stability. The long hair of the mother falls gently down the middle of the triangle, providing a decorative background against which the mother's light skin is set. The black, blue, and gold pattern of the mother's hair is at the very center of the painting *Twins* **(Fig. 42)**. The setting for this work is also Xishuangbanna. The mother kneels on the veranda of a bamboo house, rocking her boy and girl to sleep in a hammock. Black was painted over the blue in her hair for the darkest, richest tones possible. Thick black ink was used on heavily textured paper. Her red patterned skirt echoes the colors in the hammock and the roof of the Dai house in the background. In the foreground is an urn with designs based on the pottery of the prehistoric Yangshao civilization along the Yellow River.

Mother and child form an oval in the center of *Motherhood* **(Fig. 43)**, the mother's long neck curving protectively around her daughter. The mother's skirt has a pattern borrowed from gold and silver inlay designs on Han period bronze decorative arts. Ting reworked hunting scenes from Warring States-period bronzes in the background. His preoccupation with placing flat figures against a decorative background may have come from works by Matisse that he had seen in library books. The security the child feels, even with hunting scenes in the background, is related to the reassurance the mother gives the child whose father is at war in *Cradle Song* **(Fig. 41)**. The overwhelming faith Ting shows in the ability of a mother to protect her child makes one wonder how many times he longed for his absent mother during his own troubled childhood. *Tribal Kiss* also shows a mother curved protectively around her child. The skin of the figures is black against a light, wrinkled ground. Flanking the mother and child are wooden tribal sculptures from Africa, and an African mask is on the far right. Ting's interest in the tribal arts of Chinese minorities is reminiscent of Picasso's interest in primitive art. In this piece Ting pays homage to Picasso, but also reveals his fascination with different cultures and faraway places.

More recent depictions of mothers and children focus less on the protective role of the parent, and convey a sense of pleasure in each other's company. For example, mother and daughter pause in *Morning Walk* **(Fig. 44)** to share delight in some small aspect of nature. *Moonlight* **(Fig. 45)**, 1994, shows a moment of shared tranquillity and human touch at the end of a day. These two paintings are fine examples of Ting's persistent progress in the mastery of his craft. In the 1990s he has continually cultivated and refined his sense of rich color and exquisite line. In addition his figures have become more personal and expressive. The remote icons of the 1980s have developed more human characteristics.

Distant Lands

One of Ting's dreams is to travel to a new place each year, learn about the customs and absorb as much as possible of the culture, then paint what he has learned. Though he spent three months in Japan at one point, and some time in Thailand and Indonesia, he only completely realized this dream of immersion in an exotic culture in Xishuangbanna. This has not prevented him from reading about other cultures, however, and studying their art. He

has painted several pictures of African women, mesmerized by the color possibilities of black skin. He has also done works incorporating the art of India, Japan, Greece, Thailand and Bali. For example, in *Blue Diamond* **(Fig. 46)** he sets a blue-clad Indian princess in a striking contrast against a background of red Rajput princes, based on Indian paintings from the eighteenth century. *Bali Princess I* **(Fig. 47)** shows a young bride against a gold and red wedding tapestry decorated to resemble Indonesian shadow puppets.

Ting's romanticism involves not only subjects from distant lands, but also from earlier time periods. *Han Palace Light* **(Fig. 48)** shows a palace lady from the Han period leaning against bronze lamps in the shape of animals. The background is fashioned from decorative motifs from ancient bronzes.

Exotic customs also touch a romantic chord in Ting. *June Bride* **(Fig. 49)** depicts a Dai minority woman who goes to the temple to pray before her wedding. The bright red colors symbolize marriage and good fortune in China. In the circle, which is reminiscent of a railing relief from Bharhut, a celebratory dance is performed by an Indian dancer. But the background shows warrior figures inspired by ancient rock paintings that were discovered in Yunnan province in 1965.[102] While the girl prays for happiness, her future is uncertain. The bright red could also symbolize bloodshed. In this painting, as in so many others, Ting empathizes with the dreams of the girl.

Ancient Tales

Chinese myths and stories were another source of inspiration for Ting's paintings of the 1980s. Two of Ting's favorites are actually Yunnanese tales. One is the love story between Prince Zhaoshutun and the Peacock Maiden that was collected and published in the early days of the Communist regime, accompanied by Zhang Guangyu's illustrations. Yuan Yunsheng included a peacock dance in his airport mural depicting the spring festival of the Dai people, a reference to this story. Ting used peacock motifs in a number of his works. *The Peacock Princess* **(Fig. 50)** is a rendition of the heroine of the beautiful love story. The other favorite Yunnan story is that of Ashima, the girl who drowned and turned to stone while fleeing a wicked man who would have forced her to marry. Ting painted several versions of Ashima. In *Ashima at Sunrise* **(Fig. 51)** she looks like an Egyptian princess in profile with the Stone Forest and the morning sun behind her. Her warm, palpable skin has a superb textured quality to it, a blend of many layers of colors that are not easily distinguished. The skin is in contrast to the other parts of the painting where the colors are pure and bold and more easily separated one from the other. According to Ting she has already turned to stone in this picture, and the bird lights on her hands without fear.

To Ting, birds symbolize freedom. Though Ashima's story is tragic, she is nonetheless free from the tyranny of her would-be husband.

Moonlight **(Fig. 52)**, 1988, depicts another tragic story. In this tale the heroine's family is killed by a flood. As a result she hates the river and tries to kill it by filling it with earth, stones, and twigs. She spends her entire life at this task, and when she dies she becomes a bird who continues to collect tree branches and deposit them in the river. Ting fuses the bird, the girl, the river, and two moons—one crescent and one round—in a two-dimensional space. As in most of his works of the 1980s there is no fore-, middle or background. Instead the figure is placed on a flat, decorative plane. The river forms the decorative ground in this painting, covering over the moons, the bird and parts of the girl to symbolize the girl's eternal relationship with the river. The linear emphasis that is found in all Ting's works is especially dominant here. Not only are the figures drawn with long, sinuous gold lines, but each ripple of the water is also defined. His mastery of line, learned from both ancient Chinese figure painting and calligraphic brushwork, is nowhere more evident than in this work. His mastery of color is also perfected here. Thirty shades of blue combine to give the eerie, lonesome effect of moonlight.

Another blue night scene, *Night Rider* **(Fig. 53)**, is a depiction of the mythical moon goddess, Chang E. Chang E was the wife of Hou Yi, the archer who shot down nine suns to save the earth from scorching heat. Hou Yi possessed an elixir of immortality that he planned to share with his wife so they might both live together forever. Chang E ate the entire elixir without Hou Yi's knowledge and left him for paradise. According to Ting's version of the story, when she reached the land of the immortals no one would associate with her because of her selfishness, so she was banished to the moon where she leads a lonely existence. Ting is fascinated by the selfish coldness of Chang E and plans to paint a series after her story. This painting is set in the chaotic period during which her husband was shooting suns. Panic-stricken, Chang E rides wildly through the night, not knowing her direction. The horse she rides is based on the famous second-century bronze "flying horse" unearthed in Gansu Province.

The celestial turbulence that must have taken place at the time Hou Yi shot down the suns is conveyed in *The Warrior* **(Fig. 54)** and *Ten Suns* **(Fig. 55)**. Hou Yi is vigorously posed in both paintings with taut bow and strong legs. In the figure of Hou Yi, Ting captures the tremendous energy that is released each time an arrow is shot. *The Warrior* shows Hou Yi caught mid-air against a linear pattern of round suns, curling flames, wild horses, and streaming water. His dark skin glows with the reflection of the falling suns. In *Ten Suns* a light-skinned Hou Yi rides two horses through the flaming balls that fall around him. The chaotic background is defined not through line but through a mul-

titude of colors applied to crinkled paper. The horses in both paintings are patterned after the horses in Han tomb reliefs and funerary paintings.

Hunting

The theme of the hunt represents contradiction to Ting. While men and women before the agricultural age relied on hunting to live, Ting imagines that they must also have feared and respected the animals that provided them with food. His paintings of hunters represent the conflicting emotions of unwilling killers of animals. *Eyes of Prey* **(Fig. 56)** shows a contemplative huntress against a giant *taotie* mask, the ancient bronze decorative motif of an animal's face. *Phoenix* **(Fig. 57)** emphasizes the taut body of a woman holding a phoenix-headed bow high above her head with one hand as another arm long arm reaches across her body to grasp an arrow from behind her back. The decorative background is again an ancient bronze, symbol of a society that had profound respect for animals. *Warrior of Thought* **(Fig. 58)** places the hunter against a backdrop of plentiful game birds, the targets of tiny archers below. He bows his strong neck in sorrow over the killing of the animals. Often the hunting theme is portrayed only in the background, while the foreground shows a meditative woman, as in The *Hunters* **(Fig. 59)**. The hunting figures are based on decorative motifs from late Zhou pictorial bronzes. This theme of contradiction was played out in Ting's own life as he watched people betray family and friends to save themselves from harm or censure. The anguished choices people made were often wrong, but they felt compelled to protect themselves and their children.

Rivers and Seas

Ting's fascination with the theme of water began with his depictions of rivers in Xishuangbanna. The water in *Golden Sands River* (Jinshajiang, **Fig. 60**) provides a flat plane against which the huge tree and figures are placed. It covers the entire surface, shimmering with texture and varied colors, but not detracting from the exquisitely detailed rendering of the tree foliage.

The Sound of Roaring Billows **(Fig. 61)** is another depiction of Liusha River. In this painting Ting used strong colors to convey the light that he remembers shining on the backs of the women at the river at the end of day. The river water is painted vertically in order to convey its roaring sound. "If I had painted the river horizontally it would be too peaceful," explained Ting.[103] In this painting Ting commemorated the violent death of twenty-six young men who drowned in the whirlpools of the river at the time of the Dragon Boat Festival. Drunken with celebrations of their town's victory at the races, they ventured out on the river at night. When the boat hit rocks and capsized, all the men were lost. The memory of their death was especially poignant for Ting, as he was pulled out of the boat at the last minute by a government official who was aware of the danger of overloading the boat.

In China, Ting sometimes visited his older brother in the coastal city of Qinhuangdao, where he was able to wander along the seashore. When he moved to California he visited the ocean frequently, and it provided inspiration for many works. "I really love the wind, the sea and the sails," he commented. "So I often paint that theme. The ocean gives me a very strong feeling. It always heightens whatever feeling I have when I am near it. If I am joyful, I feel more joyful near the ocean. If I am sad, it deepens my sadness." *Distant Dreams* **(Fig. 62)** is typical of his popular depictions of wind-blown beauties in an ocean setting. The colorful sails of this piece were inspired by fishermen in Hong Kong who Ting watched mending their sails with different colors of cloth.

A less typical rendering of the sea shows mermaids of three races—black, white, and Asian—swimming together in their watery home **(Fig. 63)**. Delicately patterned fish float decoratively on the surface of the painting, suspended in water defined by thin silver lines and many hues of blue, yellow and pink. Their wiry thinness and whimsical placement is reminiscent of works by Paul Klee. Using softer lines and blurred colors, Ting achieved a watery effect that leans toward abstraction.

Floating Market **(Fig. 64)** combines Ting's interest in boats and water with his curiosity about other cultures. In 1988 he visited Thailand, where he was able to compare the modern Thai culture with that of the Dai people in Yunnan province, who share the same ethnic origins. Here the water is a highly decorative combination of gold, black, blues, and reds. The sharply focused boats and figures contrast with the impressionistic rendering of the water. The two women wear traditional Thai skirts, intricately detailed and colored to complement the river's hues. The cut-off boat and umbrella bring the viewer close into the picture, close enough to see the neatly arranged fruit in the baskets. Though the floating market in Thailand bustled with commerce, one hardly gets the feel of buying and selling from this work. Ting's romanticism prevails as he shows his vision of what he dreams about for himself and others. He knows that the canals of Bangkok are polluted, and that many of the women live degraded lives as prostitutes, but he shows a better world in his art. He said:

> I was especially impressed by the old culture,
> beautiful temples, and beautiful women in
> Thailand. But many of the women are prostitutes,
> which is detestable. Foreign men come to
> Thailand, and these beautiful country women are
> forced to give up the beauty and gentleness of their
> country to them. I paint what I wish were reality
> for the Thai women, rather than what is. I wish
> them to be peaceful and happy.[104]

Music

Ting believes that "music is just as important as water and air." He often includes musical instruments, both Western and Chinese, in his paintings. *The Banyan Tree in Moonlight* **(Fig. 65)** depicts a Dai woman with traditional drums and a stringed instrument. The huge roots of the banyan tree behind her symbolize the tree of life. Ting wished to make a symbolic connection between the eternal nature of music and the ancient tree. This painting is unique in that the artist did not treat the banyan tree and musical instruments as flat, decorative shapes, but gave the painting spatial depth. The woman is clearly in the foreground, and the instruments are three-dimensional objects. The tree also has volume and weight. A night scene is effectively conveyed through the use of varying shades of blue and black. In *Under the Beiye Tree* (*Dance of the Peacock*, **Fig. 66**), another play on music, body movement and trees, the rhythmic lines of background palm fronds echo the dancing limbs of a graceful woman.

In a number of works Ting painted the melody of music itself in swirling lines that envelop the figure. *Harmony* **(Fig. 67)** blends the lines of the melody with those of a harpist, cranes, the sun, and the moon. The inspiration for this painting was a harpist hired to play at an art exhibition. "Everyone was very loud and talking," explained Ting. "The woman just kept playing her harp quietly in the background. It gave me a very peaceful feeling."[105]

Dreams of Peace

The search for peace underlies nearly every theme painted by Ting Shao Kuang. After coming to the United States, he continued to paint utopian landscapes for a while, scenes of paradise based on the sketches he made for wall paintings in China. Examples of these are *Pastoral* and *Xishuangbanna* **(Figs. 68–69)**. The landscapes are descriptions of a simple and peaceful existence, places set apart from the ordinary world. But he soon developed a more individualized mode for expressing the desire for peace through single figures of young women and birds. It was these figure paintings that first brought him success in the art market. The graceful birds are his personal symbol of the freedom to pursue one's dreams. In 1984 he won the "Best of Show" award at California State University's special exhibition in honor of Dr. Martin Luther King, Jr., with his depiction of a woman contemplating her dreams in *Wings of Victory* **(Fig. 70)**. The birds that fly toward the sun seem to come directly from her thoughts, expressing hope for a bright future for herself and her people. *Wishing for Peace* **(Fig. 71)** is a portrait of the girl he loved so many years ago in Xishuangbanna. She releases two cranes into the air, reminiscent of the Asian Buddhist practice of setting captive birds free to win blessings. Again, the birds symbolize her thoughts, her hopes, and her dreams.

A Wa minority girl dreams of a happy marriage in *Purple Dreams* **(Fig. 72)**. Her wish for happiness is symbolized by the crane that lifts into the air behind the red and purple ferns that frame the girl. "Purple dream" in Chinese refers to the dream of a young girl. The brilliant plants stand out boldly against a gorgeously textured ground of black and purple flecked with gold. Ting combined both cool and warm colors in the skin of the girl so that it glows with vibrant life. The unique textures and colors of skin he achieves in his paintings give his works a captivating quality that defies photographic reproduction. Ting has painted many successful variations on the theme of women and cranes. In a number of paintings the long beaks of the cranes seem to pierce the women's bodies, as though alluding to the woman's dream of sexual happiness. But Ting refuses to admit any erotic overtones to the works. According to him artistic balance alone dictates the placement of the cranes.

East and West

In his art of the 1980s, Ting made the stylistic and theoretical influences on his work the subject of some of his paintings. *Relaxation* **(Fig. 73)** is a reference to Picasso's Les Desmoiselles d'Avignon. While none of Ting's works actually look like anything Picasso has done, he nonetheless learned a great deal from this Western master. From the cubists Ting learned to flatten body parts and recombine them in his own fashion. He learned to look at figures and objects from multiple points of view, and he learned that color is relative and does not have to relate to the natural world. *Stone Garden* **(Fig. 74)** is a reference to Matisse, who inspired Ting to experiment with integrating patterns with human form. The flat, decorative nature of Ting's recent work is related to that of Matisse. *Life Cycles* **(Fig. 75)** is based on Gustav Klimt's *The Three Ages of Women*. He used Wa minority women as models for this painting. Because of the hard work the Wa women were required to do, they were worn and broken by the time they reached forty years of age. While Ting was fascinated by this one painting by Klimt, he was less influenced by him than by the twentieth-century Italian painter Modigliani. The long necks and small, oval faces of Ting's figures are strongly reminiscent of the work of Modigliani, who presented a modern reworking of the Italian Mannerist style.

Although Ting studied and learned from the works of the modern masters Picasso, Matisse, Modigliani, Klee, Dubuffet, Dali, and Miro, the source that nourished him most directly was the decorative art of China, especially the figure paintings on the walls of temples and ancient palaces. In *Dunhuang Mural* **(Fig. 76)** he pays homage to that rich source of inspiration with a direct copy of figures from the caves. While Western masters taught him that flattened figures could be modern, he did not need to look

further than Chinese figure painting for two-dimensional patterns. The exquisite linearity of Ting's paintings also came from his study of Dunhuang art. While Ting loved the strong and unusual coloring of the Fauves and was influenced by them in his use of color, he also relied on the bright colors of ancient Chinese temple murals for inspiration. Ting's art thus owes far more to Chinese tradition than many Western viewers realize.

The painting *Silk Road* **(Fig. 77)** symbolizes Ting's combination of elements from both Eastern and Western art. The camels represent the exchange of goods and ideas between China and Western civilizations along the Silk Road long ago. Artists at Dunhuang, an important outpost on the Silk Road, were open to artistic ideas that came from the West, just as Ting is open to new stylistic influences. The background colors of the painting are reminiscent of the desert sands of Gansu province, the location of the Dunhuang caves, and beyond. The pattern of the woman's clothing is the *kuei* dragon, a motif taken from ancient Chinese bronzes. The swirling lines could be the desert winds but could also represent the blending of many artistic traditions.

Wu Guanzhong, one of the most prominent artists living in China, said, "Ting Shao Kuang has carried the blood of the East to the West. He will create a new breed of art, but it will take a long time to tell if it will succeed. He is in the beginning stages of combining eastern and western art. The challenge lies in whether or not it can endure history and time."[106] Ting Shao Kuang has indeed brought an entirely new look to Chinese painting. His technical accomplishment is nearly perfect. His mastery of line and color is unsurpassed. But the freshness of his vision must continue to develop if he is to make a lasting impact on the art world. While keenly aware of the necessity of producing works that will sell, Ting is nonetheless determined not to exchange the tyranny of censorship for the tyranny of the marketplace. Ting's early success forced him to work rapidly, sometimes repeating himself. But his recent works demonstrate that he has the strength to continue to make artistic progress, despite the demands of consumers. The story of this energetic and charismatic artist is not yet finished, but based on his past strength of character and nonconformist spirit, one can predict that he will continue to achieve new heights in his art.

New Motifs

There is already evidence in the first half of the 1990s that Ting Shao Kuang is moving in new directions. In 1992 he was one of four artists commissioned to paint works for Floriade, the International Flower Festival in Amsterdam. This commission diverted his attention from figures to flowers. Since then he has made several stunning floral compositions, such as *Flowers of Paradise* **(Fig. 78)** and

Orchids and Irises **(Fig. 79)**. In *Bountiful Harvest* **(Fig. 80)** he experimented with the combination of this new floral theme with an elegant woman for a fresh look. The painting is much more light-hearted than his earlier depictions of wistful beauties with hopeful but uncertain dreams. The woman is confident and clearly enjoys the flowers and her own beauty.

Ting has also revived his passion for landscape, despite the obvious success of his figure paintings. In 1990 he turned again to monochrome ink to create *Xishuangbanna House* and *Running Sand River* **(Fig. 81)**. He also painted a color version of *Running Sand River* **(Fig. 82)**, recreating a scene where nature provides a setting in which people can live harmoniously. Ting believes that for the most part, contemporary humans are divorced from nature, living frantic, nervous lives in urban settings, and losing their balance. His landscape paintings are an attempt to restore that lost balance. *Sacred Village* **(Fig. 83)** includes a small pagoda in the scene, but the foliage and the river still dominate. In each landscape his imagination and superb sense of coloring never fail to produce exquisite and varied renderings of trees and plants. When one compares his latest landscapes to those painted before his concentration on figures, one can see that Ting's art has matured both technically and artistically to the point that *Running Sand River* can be called a true masterpiece.

More experimentation in his figure paintings is also apparent. A certain playfulness in *Chinese New Year* **(Fig. 84)** sets one of Ting's elegant musicians against the background of a traditional New Year print. The print is replete with symbolic wishes for the coming year, including peaches for long life and pomegranates for fertility. Two boys fighting over a hat form a rebus for success in the civil service exams. In traditional China, sons who could pass the exams were the most certain means to wealth and prestige for the family. Now that Ting Shao Kuang has secured both for his own family, he can afford to pursue whatever direction his art may take him next.

Painting and the Politics of Peace: Ting Shao Kuang Represents China for the United Nations

Ting Shao Kuang's financial success has continued into the nineties, despite a worldwide recession that slowed the art market. For example, at Christie's 1991 autumn auction in Hong Kong, *White Night* **(Fig. 85)** set a new record for the highest amount ever paid to acquire a contemporary Chinese painting. During the past eleven years he has held more than three hundred one-person exhibitions in Japanese galleries. His works have also been sold for high prices at the new Jia De Auction House in Beijing. He opened his own gallery in Beverly Hills in 1995, and a second gallery in Jakarta, Indonesia, in 1997. But monetary achievement, though welcome, has not been the primary goal of Ting Shao Kuang. Rather, he has worked to achieve a sense of loving peace in his paintings that first acted as a catharsis for his own pain, and now relates the concept of a harmonious world order that he envisions for all.

In 1992, Ting became a citizen of the United States. His affluence, and the freedom citizenship afforded, enabled him to take on the role of an ambassador of peace through art, a position that brings him great satisfaction. *Peace and Friendship* **(Fig. 86)** expresses his capacity to symbolize reconciliation between East and West while celebrating their different points of view. Dressed in ancient clothing representing separate civilizations, the two women kneel together at front center and jointly release a flock of doves, the international metaphor for peace.

In 1993 *Light for Human Rights* **(Fig. 87)** was chosen by the Art and Philatelic Programme of the World Federation of United Nations Associations (WFUNA) as the first day cover for its Human Rights stamp series. In addition to the first day cover, 750 limited edition prints of *Light for Human Rights* were printed and sold by WFUNA to support its programs. In a bulletin from the United Nations Headquarters in New York dated 11 June 1993, Annabelle Wiener, Deputy Secretary General of WFUNA, announced the stamp issue and explained its significance:

> On 11 June 1993, the United Nations Postal Administration (UNPA) will issue the fifth and final set of stamps in its multi-year series commemorating the Universal Declaration of Human Rights. Launched on 17 November 1989, the Human Rights stamp series is one of the most important projects undertaken by UNPA. Now in its final year, the series continues to commemorate the hopes, efforts and achievements of people everywhere towards the universal realization of human rights and fundamental freedoms.

The Art and Philatelic Programme began in 1966 with Salvator Dali's presentation of a painting to commemorate the 20th anniversary of the United Nations. Other artists whose works have been featured on WFUNA first day covers include Marc Chagall, Alexander Calder, Andy Warhol, Joan Miro, Robert Rauschenberg and Victor Vasarely. Ting Shao Kuang is the first Chinese artist to participate in the Programme. Proceeds from the sales of the stamps and limited edition prints are used to finance WFUNA's work to promote public understanding of the United Nations.

Light for Human Rights depicts three women—one African, one Asian, and one Caucasian—with arms raised upward in a gesture of hope. Oppression is experienced by all races; women and children are the most frequent victims of violence in their own homes. Characteristically, Ting portrays not conflict, but unity among these women of different cultures; not sorrow from oppression, but the "light" of freedom from tyranny. The women gaze upward at the birds, symbols of hope, and face the sun. The African woman carries a small daughter on her back, symbolizing hope for the future. The multi-colored rays of the sun form a textured background that sets off the detailed costumes of the elegant women. The lines of the sun rays also lift the viewer's eyes upward toward the light.

The General Assembly of the United Nations proclaimed 1994 as the International Year of the Family with the following theme, "Family: resources and responsibilities in a changing world." Another of Ting Shao Kuang's paintings, *Motherhood* **(Fig. 43)**, was chosen by WFUNA for a first day cover and a limited edition set of prints commemorating the Year of the Family. On February 3, 1994 Ting presented the first of the signed, limited edition prints of *Motherhood* to then Secretary-General of the United Nations, Mr. Boutros Boutros-Ghali. In her February 4, 1994 memorandum to announce the prints to the public, Annabelle Wiener, Deputy Secretary-General, said:

> *The family assumes diverse forms and functions from one country to another as well as within each nation. The widest possible protection and assistance should be accorded to families so that they may fully assume their responsibilities within the community. In spite of the many changes in society that have altered its role and functions, the family constitutes the basic unit of society and remains a vital means of preserving and transmitting cultural values. It is in this context of social change that families must become the medium for promoting new values and behavior consistent with the rights of individual family members, notably women and children, as established by various United Nations instruments.*

About **Motherhood** she wrote:

> *[Ting Shao Kuang's] real life reverence for women translates beautifully in his painting, **Motherhood** into an image of a woman and her child that is ethereal and elegant. The viewer will delight in the rich lush colors of peach, blue magenta, gold and violet used to depict the innate bond that a mother has with her child and the unique sanctity that only she can provide.*

It is paradoxical that this perfect vision of motherhood was painted by an artist whose own family was cruelly divided by politics and war. The tender interaction between mother and child in *Motherhood* is set against a background of motifs reminiscent of ancient Chinese hunting bronzes. The mother's skirt borrows its pattern from inlaid bronzes of the Warring States period in China. Mother and daughter form a tight circle compositionally, which reinforces their unity. Thin gold lines criscross the mother's torso and bind the sleeping baby to her, as though

to represent the invisible emotional bonds that can form between a mother and her child.

In 1995 Ting Shao Kuang was commissioned to paint two more works for WFUNA, this time using the theme of The Fourth World Conference on Women, "Peace, Equality, and Development." The conference was held in Beijing in September 1995. P*eace, Equality and Development* **(Fig. 88)** was the artwork chosen for all the promotional materials for the conference. *Religion and Peace* **(Fig. 89)** was selected for the 1995 WFUNA print series. Because of the interest generated by the conference the number of limited edition prints of *Religion and Peace* was expanded from the usual 750 to 2000. Two separate editions of one thousand prints each were published, one edition of offset lithographs and one edition of serigraphs.

A stylized dove in a red disk is the focus of *Peace, Equality and Development*. The dove, a worldwide symbol of peace, is reminiscent of the intricately cut designs of various cultures—Indonesian shadow puppets, Chinese paper cuts, Belgian lace. The arms of women of diverse races stretch upward in unison toward the dove. The unity of the group is emphasized by the intertwined pattern of the women's limbs. The three women represent Europe, Africa and Asia, all centers of early human development. The patterns of their costumes are fanciful allusions to the traditional clothing worn by women of those distinct cultures. The vivid colors of the women and the dove are set against a blue and gold background of references to the art of the various centers of culture—an Egyptian wall painting, painted designs from a Greek vase, an African mask, southern Chinese bronze decor. At the bottom Ting has included his name in the form of a traditional Chinese artist's seal, but it is painted rather than stamped on his work.

In *Religion and Peace*, a kneeling woman in blue robes that are a combination of Chinese Han and minority designs sets free a dove. This refers to the Buddhist ritual in which caged birds are purchased at temples, then allowed to fly away, symbolizing release from worldly attachments. Behind the woman is a vivid temple mural painted in red. The mural is an enlarged version of an apsara, a flying celestial being who belongs to the joyful entourage of Amitabha Buddha. Ting retrieved this particular apsara from the memory of his study of the cave temples at Maijishan.

In addition to the 1995 WFUNA commission, six of Ting Shao Kuang's works were chosen for the stamps issued by the United Nations Postal Administration to celebrate The Fourth World Conference on Women. From the United Nations headquarters in New York, Deputy Secretary-General Annabelle Wiener wrote:

> *It seems altogether fitting that Mr. Ting has been commissioned to create the stamps for this most*

important UN stamp issue, given his real life reverence for women and the prominent role they play in his work.... [Ting Shao Kuang] is not only an exceptionally gifted artist, but a man to whose spirited dedication to the ideals of the United Nations Charter and fervent compassion for humanity we are deeply indebted.

Three of the stamps were new works made for the UN Postal Commission: *Freedom and Happiness* **(Fig. 90)**; *Peace, Equality and Development*, also used by WFUNA **(Fig. 88)**; and *Culture and Education* **(Fig. 91)**. The other three were chosen from previous works: *Lullaby* **(Fig. 92)**; *Wings of Victory*, the winner of the Martin Luther King Prize in 1984 **(Fig. 70)**; and a section of *Xishuangbanna* **(Fig. 93)**.

Freedom and Happiness **(Fig. 90)** shows an Egyptian woman seated next to a gigantic imaginary stringed instrument. Cranes stretch their elongated necks upward, symbolizing freedom in flight. The musical instrument represents happiness. The woman's red and gold figure forms a dramatic contrast to the swirling blue textured background of the painting. The swirls convey emotion; they are a visual rendering of the feelings of freedom and happiness that should be part of every woman's life.

A woman reading is depicted in *Culture and Education* **(Fig. 91)**. She sits on marble steps next to a pond, absorbed in a book, framed by exquisitely detailed flora. Two swans glide by in the foreground, their blue-white feathers reflecting the color of the woman's skin. Her dress is reminiscent of ancient Greece, an allusion to the foundation of Western culture. These three new compositions reveal Ting's treasured ideals for his own life—freedom, happiness, peace, equality, development, culture and education. Through his paintings he expresses his wish that those ideals might extend to all women in every culture.

Mr. Li Zhaoxing, Representative of the People's Republic of China to the United Nations, arranged for the six stamps to be printed in China, a first for China's printing industry. They were issued from Singapore September 5, 1995, at a gathering of the World Philactic Society.

Ting's artistic contributions toward world peace have been matched by community service in the form of speeches, scholarships to young artists, and leadership in various organizations. He has received commendations for his service by numerous cities in the form of certificates, keys to the city, and proclamations of "Ting Shao Kuang Day." Some of the cities include Santa Fe, New Mexico; Mexicali, Mexico; Manila, the Philippines; Los Angeles, Monterey Park, El Monte, Alhambra, Arcadia, Mountain View, Millbrae, and Los Angeles County, California. In 1993 he received Outstanding Chinese-American Role Model awards from the Orange County Chinese Cultural Club and Pan Pacific Performing Arts, Inc.

On March 5, 1992, Ting organized the Chinese Artists Association, U.S.A. in Los Angeles, with more than a hundred members, and was unanimously elected president. To celebrate the third anniversary of the organization, the members held an exhibition in Monterey Park and changed its name to the World Association of Chinese Artists. Ting was again elected president, and arranged group exhibitions in Taipei in 1994 and Mexicali, Mexico in 1995. The purpose of the association is to encourage and support Chinese artists living abroad. Its goals echo those of Shen She at the end of the Cultural Revolution.

Ting's pecuniary triumphs and his renown in the Western world made him a celebrity in China, where 25 years earlier he was once persecuted for his art. Twelve years after emigrating to the U.S., he returned to China as a guest of the government. The state sponsored exhibitions of his work in both Beijing and Shanghai in the fall of 1992. In Beijing the exhibition was held in the Central Hall of the National Historical Museum of the Revolution located on Tiananmen Square between the Forbidden City and the mausoleum of Mao Zedong. Ting was the first, and so far only, living artist ever to be granted a one-person show at this prestigious site. A forty-foot banner announcing the exhibition was draped on the front of the building, and more than 100,000 people attended the show. More than 500 articles about Ting appeared in Chinese newspapers, many with the headline TING SHAO KUANG FEVER (*Ding Shaoguang re*). China Central Television accompanied Ting throughout his stay.

While in China, Ting Shao Kuang made an emotional return to his old home in Shanxi Province. He was met at the railroad station by the vice-governor of the province and other officials. People with flowers crowded the road, making it impossible for the limousine to drive away from the station. When Ting saw security forces physically push people to clear the way, he left the car and walked the ten kilometers to his destination, leaving the officials no choice but to trail along behind him. The exuberant welcome continued in Shanghai. After the ribbon cutting to open the exhibition at the Shanghai Art Museum, an enthusiastic crowd stormed the exhibition hall, breaking the glass in the entrance and grabbing at Ting for autographs.

A banquet with over 400 guests was hosted by Ting Shao Kuang in the Great Hall of the People during the exhibition, another singular honor not previously granted to an artist. The location of the banquet was especially significant to Ting Shao Kuang because it was held in the very room that he had helped to decorate in 1980, just prior to his departure from China. In addition to officials from the Bureau of Culture, several hundred artists were also invited, including all those affiliated with the Central Academy of Art and Craft, the Central Academy of Fine Arts, and the Beijing Painting Academy. No one refused to come, even bitter rivals among the artists. The gathering was truly momentous for the many artists who had been victimized by the Cultural Revolution.

While in China Ting Shao Kuang spoke to art students in various settings, including a speech at the Guangdong Academy of Fine Arts. He also set up a scholarship in the name of his first teacher, Zhang Guangyu, for a student to attend the Central Academy of Art and Craft. He was named honorary curator of the Art Museum he established for Pang Xunqing, another teacher, in Changshu, Jiangsu Province. And the Bureau of Culture set up a national competition for a Ting Shao Kuang Award, open to any person in any medium. Letters announcing the award were sent to every county, rather than to the art academies, so that any person could apply regardless of his or her affiliation with a particular school. Whether in China or the U.S., Ting is generous and unaffected, looking for ways to promote younger artists. Even in Japan he donated his honoraria for university lectures to overseas Chinese students at Japanese institutions.

In addition to the huge painting in the Great Hall of the People, tapestries designed by Ting Shao Kuang have been installed in two new government buildings on Tiananmen Square. Both buildings belong to the All-China Women's Federation *(fu lian)*, and were designed by women. One is the organization's headquarters, the other is a Women's Activities Center. *Running Sand River* **(Fig. 82)**, which can be considered Ting's masterpiece to this point, and *Motherhood* **(Fig. 43)** were chosen by the Women's Federation for the tapestry designs, and were hung inside the new buildings just prior to the opening of the Fourth Annual Conference on Women in Beijing. In 1998, a decorative mural commissioned by the Shanghai Museum will be installed in a permanent location in the museum's newly built headquarters. Less than twenty years after giving up the coveted airport mural commission, and leaving China without recognition for his work in the Great Hall of the People, Ting Shao Kuang has come full circle as a celebrated public works artist in China.

CHAPTER SIX

THEORIES OF ART: A Conversation With Ting Shao Kuang

TING SHAO KUANG has very definite ideas about art and what it should be. As a young teacher in China he enthusiastically introduced his ideas to his students. When strict censorship made teaching his own theories difficult he turned to private evening discussions with artist friends. Even after emigrating to the West, Ting still takes great delight in leading lively discussions about art. This chapter is comprised of quotations gathered from various conversations about art that the author has held with the artist, followed by Ting's answers to a number of specific questions about his theories of art.

As an artist, Ting has two goals of primary importance. The first is to revitalize and modernize Chinese painting. The second is to create a kind of art that can be appreciated by all people, both the connoisseur and the viewer with no artistic background. He disagrees with artists who think their art is valuable only if it is inaccessible to those of common intellect. The Chinese phrase *yasu gongshang*, "appreciated by both the refined and the common," is one he uses to describe the type of art he would like to make. The ideas below are related to these goals.

Line

"At one point I painted Michelangelo's sculpture, interpreting it with lines. It is very difficult to paint something like that only with lines, without shading, light, or three-dimensionality. But it still had a sculptural feeling.

"After I had been in Xishuangbanna for a while [during his first visit there as a student] I didn't want to return. At the end of my stay I felt that I could paint every blade of grass, every flower and tree. Each plant had its own unique quality and each plant could be painted individually. Everything was beautiful to me, and I felt I could draw it all meticulously, carefully, in great detail. If I returned now I doubt I could do that. It was a very important period in my life. If you can see tranquility in my present painting it stems from the peace I felt at that time. I gave everything a very firm outline; everything was drawn clearly. It was an important process in the development of my ability to work with line. I used line to give firm, clear shapes to everything.

"Line is the soul of Chinese art. Chinese art theories about line are much more profound than Western theories of line. Line has shape, texture, and feeling. It is the basic principle of beauty in Chinese painting.

"When I paint I feel that the line must come first. My paintings are complete before I add the color. What I want to say in painting I say first with line. If the line is not good, I don't add color."

Color

"In general there are two ways to learn color. For the artist, one way is to learn directly from nature. The other method is subjective, to learn from oneself. Yunnan school artists [the modern heavy colorists] use both these methods. Colors can be changed from the objective colors of nature to the subjective colors you choose yourself. You should first learn the colors of nature, then you can change them to suit yourself. Academic painting *(xueyuanpai)* only follows nature. I don't paint trees green because I don't like green. I paint them blue, but they have the feel of green.

"Color should follow shape, but a lot of artists don't know this. Klimt sometimes has this problem. When the shape changes, the color should change too. Klee doesn't have this problem. When his shapes change, his colors change. Some artists in the Yunnan school also have this problem. Their shapes change, but their colors do not.

"I have talked about the color gold before. If the gold is right it will help the other colors. But if used in the wrong way it can eat the colors. You can't use too much or it will turn out wrong. The Japanese only know how to use one color of gold. But the shade of gold one uses must be consistent with other colors in the painting.

"Each nationality has its own feeling about color. So does each artist. I especially like blue because it represents tranquility. I can only paint when everything is quiet."

Control

"I don't like happenings or accidental feelings in art. I don't like art that is out of control. An artist must be consciously in control of his techniques, his methods, and his feelings. Picasso believed this too. This way one can control the quality of his paintings."

The Artist's Character

"After one reaches a certain age, his art is no longer a matter of technique. It is a matter of personal temperament and feeling, a matter of internal richness. If you are rich inside you can express yourself deeply on paper. If you are empty inside, your paintings will be superficial. One cannot get this from just painting. One needs to read books, experience life, and learn from other cultures. I think the many books I read during my youth have helped me to have a greater understanding of the world and its people, and has in turn made my art more meaningful."

"The artist should reach his inner world through many experiences, both direct and indirect. This is what Dong Qichang (1555–1636) called 'walking ten thousand miles and reading ten thousand books.'

"For art, one way to learn is from experience and the other is from books. You must travel and read widely to enrich your inner vision. Then you can try to find your own style, a way of expression that is unique to you. When you begin walking as a student, maybe many will go with you. But later you will go alone.

"As a student, if you do not restrict yourself you will later be restricted in what you can do. You should force yourself to conform to the principles of nature until you have mastered them. You must learn to comply with all the principles of brush and ink, color and line. The more pressure you put on yourself as a student, the more artistic freedom you will have in the future. There is a Chinese proverb that says the most successful person gets his reward when he is old. A small building is built quickly, but a large building needs time. Don't think you're great when you are young. You need to push yourself.

"I am not surprised either by lavish praise or by severe criticism. I try to remain aloof from both. But in fact, praise is far more dangerous than criticism. Successful people should take care to be modest, for too much praise can cause them to falter. If they fall because of praise, they will not stand up again. On the other hand, if one sees his weakness he can correct it and progress forward.

"When I was criticized during the Cultural Revolution I was devastated at first. That kind of criticism is not helpful. But somewhere I found the inner strength to believe in myself despite what others said. I feel now that this is once again a dangerous time for me as an artist, but for the opposite reason. I need to continue to learn despite my financial success."

How is your art related to the traditional art of China?

"I have been painting for more than forty years, since I was eleven. From the time I was in primary school to the time I became a professional artist I studied traditional Chinese art and Western art history repeatedly. Then I carefully made comparisons. Even now I like to go back and review art history because my viewpoint continues to change. I believe one must know the past well. But I don't want to resurrect the past. The purpose of studying art history is to find ways to move forward.

There are three important things I have inherited from Chinese tradition. The first is my theoretical basis. Chinese art theory has a long history, more than two thousand years. The soul of Chinese art theory is that one should pursue spiritual likeness rather than formal likeness. Gu Kaizhi (ca.344–406) said, 'Form is embodied in spirit. The spirit and the form should be combined.' He also said, "I painted this painting myself." This sentence indicates that ancient Chinese painters emphasized creative self-expression. Xie He (early 6th c.) said, 'To resemble nature is to get something from your heart.' The point is that one learns from nature, but the painting comes from one's heart. Again, this is an expression of the ancients' belief in the individuality of the painter. There is another saying from Chinese art theory: 'In human relations one must not be self-centered. But in painting, one must think only of oneself. Only then can he become a master.'

"These Chinese theories have helped me a great deal. They are not only opposed to the artist becoming a slave of nature, which is the path of the modern academic school in China, but they are also opposed to the method of copying which has dominated Chinese art history for several hundred years. Opposition to these two approaches is the theoretical basis for my painting. It is very clear to me that a successful artistic style is the result of being loyal to oneself. One cannot simply accept the ancestors' aesthetics nor copy the ancestors' techniques.

"The second thing I have learned from Chinese tradition is the use of line. The third is color. I learned color from China, not from the West. The color in ancient Chinese painting seeks harmony in strong, clear contrasts. You can see it in the figure paintings and the bird-and-flower paintings of the Tang and Song periods. Zhang Guangyu and Pang Xunqin taught that the essence of traditional Chinese art has been fading since the Yuan dynasty, but one can still see vibrant Chinese colors in Beijing opera. Chinese architecture preserves strong colors too in its red walls and green tiles. The strong colors I use in my paintings come from my study of old Chinese art."

One of the most important issues for Chinese artists today is how to respond artistically to influences from the West. Why is this an issue, and how have you dealt with it in your art?

"The correct way to study Western art is to study its theory. There is no hope for the Chinese artist who imitates Western art. I stand at a place where I can turn my head and look at the ideas of Western art, then choose from them what I think is important. That's the way I learn from Western art."

Why do you think that dealing with Asian influences is not a major issue for Westerners?

"I think the twentieth century is the great age of cultural exchange. Before this time communication was difficult. The influence of East on West should be addressed by Western artists rather than by me. What they learn I think they can answer, but I cannot answer for them."

Are there still basic differences between Chinese and Western approaches to art?

"Art has its own national character. Different groups have their own special aesthetic points of view. But there is really no gap between Eastern and Western art. All art expresses the nature of human beings. The nature of human beings is the same everywhere. Wu Guanzhong and Li Keran spoke of artists from East and West climbing the same mountain, but from different sides. Neither can see each other on the way up, but when they reach the top they are in the same place. At the pinnacle, art is universal."

The painting and calligraphy of China's literati tended toward abstraction as early as the eighth century. Why do you think total abstraction was never achieved?

"The fate of Chinese artists has always been controlled by censorship, either from civil officials or from society itself. I believe China once had pure abstract art. Though the paintings don't survive there are many stories that point to abstraction. For example, there is a story about Liang Kai [thirteenth century], who painted a feeling, not a form or a shape, one time when he was drunk. This is something like Picasso's saying, 'I painted the smile of the cat, but I didn't paint the cat.' Liang Kai said the same thing, 'painted a mountain, but you cannot see that it is a mountain.' There was another artist, Wang Xia [c. 740–804], who splashed ink on paper without a brush when he was drunk. He used his hands, feet, hair or other body parts to paint abstract shapes. There was no status for that kind of artist, however. Government officials did not give them the patronage they needed to do that kind of art, so it disappeared. Chinese did have abstract art, but it has been obliterated from history.

"Currently in world art I think there are two approaches. One favors abstraction, the other favors the figurative. The masterpieces of the next century will find a way to combine both. There is tension between abstraction and realism, but the two approaches to art depend on each other. A true artist must be capable of both. Many artists have good ideas but they have no technical skill. They don't take the time to work hard and achieve perfection; they try to cover technical flaws with abstraction. This is especially a problem with art students who want to sell their paintings before they know how to do them. You can see both technique and cultural understanding beneath the abstract works of a real artist."

What do you think are the important trends in American art?

"I will probably give you an indirect answer. In American art education, based on my teaching experience at UCLA extension and on my contacts with various students, I think freedom of expression is emphasized over fundamentals. This is a big problem. There is not enough basic training in the foundations of art in the United States. There is also a perceived contradiction between realistic and abstract art that causes problems for American art students. Some artists think that realistic painting is the opposite of abstract painting and has nothing to do with it. If they are abstract painters, they don't think they need to learn realistic painting. I think they are very wrong. Picasso studied realistic painting first, then progressed toward abstraction. He moved back and forth between the two modes. Each time the abstraction was different from the last time and each time the realistic art was different. One built on the other, and each time his art progressed. I think artists must learn both. If an artist knows only one thing he will not be a good artist.

"There are two extremes in American art. One is full abstraction and the other is photographic realism. There should be something in the middle of these two extremes. One reason the 'Yunnan school' painters are successful in the United States might be because they incorporate both abstract forms and realism.

"America also has conceptual art, which is contradictory to technique. It is not possible to have art without technique."

What do you see as your contribution to modern art?

"I think I have brought a new aesthetic point of view to America in the combination of Western and Eastern art. In the past the Chinese artists brought the old, traditional culture to America. But I bring that culture from a new point of view."

What is the "Yunnan school"?

"The Yunnan school is a lively rebellion against Chinese academic official art. But it is not a purely political movement, and thus should be distinguished from the Star Stars. The Star Star group had more political overtones. Yunnan school artists were concerned about the quality of art. They were not simply trying to imitate the West."

What is the difference between the works you did in China and the works you do here?

"I think my theory of painting is still the same here as it was in China. But in America I have had the chance to know another world culture, so my subject matter and aesthetic view have broadened. My goal in China was to form a new kind of art based on all the various cultures of the world. I tried to do this a long time ago. The earliest way for me to do this was through literature. I came to understand the joys and sorrows of many different people by reading world literature. My ideas have been fully realized in the United States. People like my work because it reflects many different cultures. My thoughts have not changed, but opportunities to develop my art have changed."

Is there a political content to your work?

"No. There are religious overtones, but no political content. The ancient philosophy of China is also in my work. I pursue beauty, truth, and gentleness, not political ideas."

What forms the theoretical basis for your works?

"I think I discussed this in the first question. I want to find a new road between abstract art and realistic art. As an artist in the modern world one should have two basic techniques. One is to surpass other people's eyes and have the ability to see beyond what others can see. To be able to see details and describe them in a profound way. More than just painting the outward appearance of a tree, I want to be able to convey its feelings. The other is a sense of line. One must know the movement of abstract line and color. It is this movement that embodies emotional form. One must have both of these—first a detailed study and knowledge of the subject, and then the abstract line to convey feeling. I think twentieth century abstract art is very important because it opened half the door. I want to learn what the abstract expressionists learned, but I want to go a different way."

Why do idealized women dominate the subject matter of your works?

"I will give a very simple answer. I think humans already have enough turmoil. I should keep pain to myself and give beauty to the world. I think women are beautiful and they make my paintings beautiful."

What is it that you most wish to express with your art?

"I want to express the essence of human nature. Things such as love and motherhood. I think these are the permanent subjects for humanity. Sometimes artists want to express the simplicity of life, even though the world is quite complicated. Religions might have very thick books to explain their philosophies, but it can all be expressed in one sentence, 'Do good.' Art is like that too. It can be simple, yet profound. I want to express what is simple and eternal."

What artistic direction do you wish to take in the future?

"The direction I wish to take is to find an avenue between abstract art and realistic art. To combine Western and Eastern art and make a new contribution with this."

[Don't you feel you have already achieved this?]

"No. I have a long way to go. There is a Chinese proverb: 'It doesn't matter if you go slowly, as long as you don't stand still.'"

EASTERN AND WESTERN ART

A Lecture Presented by Ting Shao Kuang to the Los Angeles Fine Arts Council, 1993

TO UNDERSTAND THE POSITION Chinese painting holds in the world today, one must first comprehend the history and development of both Chinese and Western art. From the beginning, the two sides of the world have followed divergent paths in their approaches to art. Western art followed the model of ancient Greece, seeking the unification of pure art and science. The sculpture of ancient Greece is very realistic because it is based on scientific methods. Renaissance artists continued the development of precise anatomy, perspective and color theory. This approach led to the appreciation of realism in Western art.

The path Chinese art followed, however, was not based on scientific imitation of a three-dimensional world. The first of Xie He's *Six Rules for Painting*, written in the fifth century, was that "the atmosphere must be alive." Other ancient treatises followed his lead in regarding "spirit" as the most important criterion for a work of art. In other words, what ancient Chinese artists were seeking in their works was "spirit" and not just "form." From the beginning, the path of Chinese art was one of understatement, symbolism, and distortion, of manipulating the form to describe the spirit. This applied even to sculpture. The sculpted figures in Chinese temples are monumental, but not anatomically correct. This is different from Western sculpture, but one cannot say that the starting point of Chinese art is somehow lower than that of the West. On the contrary, the ability to rise above form demonstrates the brilliance of Chinese art. Ancient medical texts verify that the Chinese understood anatomy very well. It was not through lack of knowledge, but by choice that Chinese artists emphasized spirit over form. In art, correct anatomy was not a criterion for evaluation.

The Four Major Periods in Western Art

There are four dominant periods in Western art. The first is that of ancient Greece. Artists in the following ages were unable to recreate the art of the Greeks. Why is this so? One reason is that the physical environment of Greece and what the Greeks sought to express artistically are strongly connected. The age of the ancient Greeks was like the springtime of the human race. People viewed beauty with an almost mystical reverence, the same reverence given to the gods. A person with a beautiful physique or superior athletic ability was given a godlike status, and revered without jealousy. Because of this veneration of physical beauty, this was the age of the nude in art.

According to records of the time, there were at least as many sculptures as there were people. Nearly every person was an artist, each with an integral concept of beauty. The unclothed human body was recognized as pure and natural during this idealistic period, creating a high point in the development of art. Behind this respect for beauty were strict requirements for anatomical proportions: the head should be one-eighth of the overall height, the length of the palm two-thirds the height of the head, the upper arm one head-length, the lower arm one-and-a-half head-lengths, and so on. Artists in the Middle Ages might have been capable of using these formulas, but they were unable to enter the state of pure appreciation of the human body. The times had changed; the artist's environment had changed.

The second high point in Western art is the Italian Renaissance of the fourteenth and fifteenth centuries. Works such as Dante's Inferno fostered ideas of self-cultivation, humanitarianism, and equality of all persons before God, challenging the strict hierarchy of the Middle Ages. Michelangelo was the greatest of all the Renaissance artists. Rodin summarized the impact of the art of ancient Greece and fifteenth-century Italy when he wrote, "Youth who love beauty, you should bow down and show respect for Polykleitos and Michelangelo. Esteem the godlike solemnity of the former and the rough melancholy of the latter."

The third major period in Western art history is the nineteenth century. Of the many important artists who emerged at this time, Delacroix, who played a crucial role in the development of the use of color, is perhaps the most innovative. Before Delacroix, the main emphasis was on drawing. Color was almost an afterthought, added to the outline. Delacroix, however, used color directly to create form and shape. He used color in place of drawing, and when he had finished painting, the line and color of his shapes were decided at the same time. At one point in his career, Delacroix painted nonstop for four days and nights to complete *The Massacre at Chios*. He then invited Ingres, who led the movement that drawing was essential to form in art, to see the painting. At first, Ingres and some of his group were impressed with the life-like depiction of the bloody scene. But as they moved closer to the painting, they discovered that the whole was nothing but brushmark after brushmark of color, completely different from the surface of traditional paintings. Ingres then said that

Delacroix didn't understand how to draw, and should go back to learn how to draw correctly. Delacroix responded cleverly: "From that close you can't see my painting's good points. You should stand behind me and then look." The double meaning in his response was that Ingres' artistic achievement had already fallen behind his own.

The fourth high point in Western art history is in the first part of the twentieth century when art reached an unprecedented peak in terms of the number of artists and the emergence of varied styles. The development of photography, and other technological advances, had a great influence on this profusion of new styles. Prior to the invention of photography in the nineteenth century, the primary means of recording a person's image was through painting or sculpture. Society's demand for portraiture strengthened the position of the sculptor or painter. After its invention, however, photography began to take over the artist's role as portrait maker. Artists' creative response to the camera's ability to capture images was to originate styles that could not be replaced by photographs. This innovation was the source of the development of modern art.

In their search for new directions, European artists sometimes turned to exotic cultures for inspiration. Gauguin's retreat to Tahiti is one well-known example. The impressionists were heavily influenced by their discovery of Japanese woodblock prints. Picasso and Modigliani learned new approaches from African tribal art. After centuries of isolated development, the arts of East and West actively mingled in the minds of artists, and presaged the great age of interaction between Eastern and Western cultures.

The Development of Chinese Art History: Form and Spirit

Chinese painting reaches three thousand years into the past. The earliest extant paintings in China date back to the third and fourth centuries. Even at that time, there were fully developed theoretical treatises on art, indicating that Chinese painting already had a long tradition. Personal expression was valued from the beginning of Chinese painting. The fourth century artist Gu Kaizhi wrote, "I paint what I feel; spirit and form are all in what I see." He also said, "It is easy to play the musical strings, but to watch the swan flying away is difficult," and "Paint your magnificent feelings." I have already mentioned the early Chinese preference for spirit over form. The value placed on the artist's expression of his feelings is another important early characteristic of Chinese art.

Two extraordinary monuments of Chinese art have made a profound impression on my own artistic development. One is the Mogao caves near Dunhuang that comprise a massive twenty-five kilometer long "gallery" containing the art of eleven dynasties. The other is the cave temples at Maijishan, which has some of the best surviving

sculpture from various periods of China's history. The sculptor Rodin kept copies of two Maijishan figures from the Wei dynasty, the boy and girl from Cave 102, in his sitting room. Though he had casts of well-known pieces from every period of Western art, these Chinese genre figures were the only works displayed in the room. The famous Mexican artist, Siquieros, was also moved by Chinese sculpture. When he saw the monumental Buddha of Yungang Cave 20, he knelt before it, stating that a person could not stand in the presence of such great art. I heard this story for the first time at the age of sixteen, and it made a strong impression on me. I deeply felt the truth of his statement, and began to realize the rich legacy of ancient Chinese art, not just for China, but for the world.

But our artistic heritage can also be a burden if not used properly. For example, far too much emphasis was traditionally placed on literati painting. Literati painting is important in China's history, but it is only one part of the overall picture. Buddhist art and folk art are also highly significant. Art education in China has been biased toward literati painting. The worst example of Chinese art education is the use of *The Mustard Seed Garden Manual*. I don't know how many art talents have been lost because of the fear of breaking the rules set forth in this manual. When following the rules of this book to teach Chinese Painting I feel that behind me stands the whole line of my ancestors, this one saying "hold the brush like this," that one telling me "bamboo must be painted like this." You can't use this type of manual to teach students. It deadens you and ties your hands—you've no way to even move your brush.

There are accounts of artists who fought against the dogmatic methods taught in painting manuals. The story of Chen Laolian studying painting is a good example. After Chen Laolian had studied with his teacher for three months, someone told him that his paintings could pass for his teacher's paintings. This was meant as a compliment, but Chen was very angry and went straight back to practice painting again. Three months later people said that his paintings were completely different from his teacher's, and he was extremely happy. Why did Chen succeed? It is because, from the beginning, he was different. He knew that the creation of art must demonstrate one's individuality.

Before the Yuan dynasty each artist had his own characteristics and style. The styles of early artists such as Wu Daozi, Gu Kaizhi, Zhou Fang and others are all clearly distinguishable. If we look at painters after the Yuan dynasty, however, with the exception of a few very successful masters, all have styles very similar to each other. For six hundred years, painters from the literati class concentrated on monochrome ink painting and did not care for colors. They abandoned half of the expressive power of painting. Certainly, monochrome painting is beautiful, but not every artist should paint that way. There should be recognizable distinctions among the styles of individual artists.

When I was teaching at UCLA, I showed some faculty and students paintings done over a period of about three hundred years in early modern China. After they had looked at them, I asked: "What do you think?" They answered that all these must have been painted by one person. I said that there were at least a hundred painters in these works, but no matter how much I talked and explained, few could tell the difference. They thought the styles were similar to each other. The paintings were of one philosophy, one aesthetic taste, one type of composition, one type of brush work and one type of craft. With this type of repetition, it is no wonder that stylistic advances came more and more slowly. Early Chinese artists didn't repeat themselves like the later literati painters did. An eighth century art theorist said, "When associating with people and handling affairs, there can be no 'I'. But when painting, everywhere is 'I'." Early artists believed strongly in the expressionistic possibilities of art.

It is astonishing how closely ancient Chinese treatises on painting coincide with contemporary art theory and the needs of modern artists. The irony is that Chinese artists stopped listening to their own voices just when their ideas began to appeal to the outside world. In the nineteenth and twentieth centuries Asians began to learn from Westerners. However, we didn't learn the best from them. Instead, we tried to reform Chinese painting with traditional Western perspective and anatomy. As a result, we lost the spiritual essence of Chinese painting. At a time when Westerners were discarding their traditions, turning to the East for creating modern art, we were taking home the trash they had thrown away. What a strange phenomenon!

The Value of Art Is in Creation

After the Yuan dynasty, a strongly conservative trend in painting that lasted several hundred years caused a decline in the quality of art. A deficient art education was the culprit. The major problem with art education was that students were required to imitate their masters. The master was under the mistaken impression that the more painters who followed his style, the greater he was as an artist and teacher. In reality, art isn't like science where one plus one equals two. The value of art lies in creation. The life blood of art depends on creativity. Art is creation.

If a master is able to teach ten students to have ten different styles, he is the best teacher. If the styles of the ten students all look the same as that of the teacher, this teacher is incompetent. So are his students. There are too many such cases. Once, a well-known Chinese painter took five of his students to Japan for an exhibition. The students he picked painted exactly like he did. After the show, both he and his students were finished. No one could tell the difference between them.

Another traditional aspect of Chinese painting that should be abandoned is collaborative paintings. If the painting is done by three or four artists just to commemorate an occasion, this is valid as a historical document. But from an artistic standpoint, collaboration goes against the nature of artistic creation. How can three or four people share the same soul? In a minute, there appear rocks, bamboo and flying birds and a painting is done. This really is just cheapening art. If artists wish to work collaboratively, the two artists must be able to interact spiritually. If they sketch together and step by step form a collaborative relationship, blending their states of mind, then it might work. But a spontaneous collaborative performance vulgarizes art, reducing it to the level of technical skill alone.

Painting the Feelings of the Soul: "I don't paint the cat itself, I paint its smile."

It's very important in art to separate technique and skill; these are two completely different things. Having technique does not necessarily mean you have skill. It's like comparing Gai Jiaotian's somersaults with those of his students. The technique of his young students is great, they turn somersaults like gymnasts. Gai Jiaotian is not as nimble as they are, but he acts as the real hero Wu Song. His poses on stage are perfect from every angle. It is just as when some people play the piano. They may have great techniques—not a note is wrong—but when you listen, there is no flavor. With good pianists, playing is a creative process, they can enter a mood or a feeling. Some artists may be very good in terms of technique, but in terms of their creative artistic skill, I think, they need to work harder.

An important aspect of Western art of the twentieth century is that the artist is not necessarily painting what he sees in the world, but is painting the world as it has been experienced by his own soul. He digests what he has seen, then recreates what he feels at heart. Picasso said, "I don't paint the cat itself, I paint its smile." To me this sentence is wonderfully mysterious. A cat's smile can be interpreted in countless artistic expressions, all a step beyond just painting its shape.

The Chinese had this perspective on art many centuries ago. From the earliest times, Chinese artists were encouraged to paint the feelings of the soul. "Within your heart should be a thousand mountains and ten thousand lakes," was a commonly quoted phrase among Chinese artists. In the twentieth century Westerners reached the point where the primary purpose of art was to express the feelings of the soul. Form and objective representations of reality became less important than expressing the inner, subjective world of the artist. This is the reason that so many varied schools and artistic categories were created in the twentieth century.

Modern artists of the West have absorbed nourishment from Eastern art, closing the gap between Eastern and Western art. The Chinese artist Wu Guanzhong assessed the situation with this analogy: "Eastern and Western artists are like two mountain climbers, one climbing from the East, the other climbing from the West. At the journey's midpoint, because the mountain is in the way, they can't see each other, yet when they reach the summit, they will definitely come together." Human nature guarantees that artists from different parts of the world share some things in common. As climbers seeking the same mountain top, the goals of Eastern and Western artists combined will lead to a pinnacle in the history of art.

The Merging of Eastern and Western Art: The East and The West; Realism and Abstraction; The Classical and The Modern

There are two kinds of artists, regional and international. Regional artists reflect the special character of their own nation. International artists cannot hope to become masters until they have studied and absorbed influence from various cultures in the world. Improved transportation and communications in the twentieth century have provided the means through which artists can conceivably become international masters. Indeed, there are already artists who have transcended cultural limits to make art that speaks to the entire world.

An emerging world culture has its critics, to be sure. The French critic Andre Parinaud has raised many questions about what world culture will mean in the twenty-first century. Even the fear that commerce will destroy civilization has been voiced. Philosophers inevitably ponder the future of art in a world economy.

The economic depression of the last few years has been a time of great challenge to artists and the art market. Galleries went bankrupt, and even works by well-known artists went unsold. As a result, gallery owners and artists have both raised the question: when the new high tide approaches, what will art be like? What kind of art will become the paragon, the representation of the time? Of course in times of difficulty, those artists who have not fallen by the wayside may become the representatives of this new art, but some new emerging artists will be representative, too.

I often discuss these questions about what art will be like in the future with friends. Speaking frankly, no matter how much we discuss it, I think you can divide all of the world's trends, styles and schools into two fundamental factions. One group has forms, images and realistic shapes. What is painted is what can be seen. The other is abstract and formless. Artists, however, will often stand on one side and fight against the other. Realists feel that abstract painting is too willful, crazy, or disorderly.

Abstract painters feel that they are more modern and that realism has fallen behind the times, is too conservative or old fashioned. Often they adopt an antagonistic attitude toward each others' works. I feel that today's artists should not be antagonistic towards these two ideas, but should be inclusive. In reality, several established modern schools, such as the American surrealists, use abstract art concepts to paint realistic subjects. The paintings of Dali are good examples. The overall feeling of his paintings is abstract, although every detail he paints is realistic, and the technique is concrete.

In my opinion, the master painter of the future will be one who is able to combine both Eastern and Western approaches, both classical and contemporary ideas of beauty, and both realism and abstraction all in the same style. This is a difficult goal, but it is what I hope some of us will accomplish. To express all the elements of painting at once is my idea of success in the twenty-first century.

Style: Faithful to Your Inner Feelings Without Reservation

I would also like to talk about how style is developed. We all know that an artist must have his own distinctive style. I feel that the development of a style is the result of an artist's faithfulness to his own feelings without reservation. You cannot take another artist's style and turn it to your own style. That is to say, it is impossible to turn Picasso's style into a new style of your own. That is a dead end.

To be faithful to your own feelings without reservation requires many types of nourishment to supplement your ideas. Simply painting every day, or practicing basic skills every day will not take you there. You must read; you must watch movies; you must travel; you must associate with learned masters and make good friends. The refined artistic talents of a person are the result and synthesis of every type of cultivation. When everything comes together, you will develop a feeling which you are unable to express through anything that has been done before. Oil painting won't do it. Neither will traditional Chinese painting. Another person's techniques will not help. It is at this time that you have hope. You've found something that's special, internal, and that you've never discovered before. You must persist now and discover the means through which you can express your feelings. Zheng Banqiao said: "When you paint something new, you are painting what you know." What he talks about is in this realm.

When you feel that you don't know what to paint, this is also the time that you have hope. It is at the time you feel you can no longer express yourself adequately that you are about to make an artistic or technical breakthrough. You are forced to select a method and think of a way to express in paint your inner experience. The things you paint at this time will most certainly have new artistic worth because it will be your own new style. All the great masters in history have had new ideas, whether in theory, technique, or personal aesthetics. It was only from this point on that they had the potential to become significant contributors to art.

Once the new style, or means of expression, has been developed, the best and most intelligent artist will spend years to digest it. You cannot paint three paintings and then change your style or approach. You must spend ten years or more continuously exploring your new idea, taking it to its deepest level, until you feel there is nothing left to paint. Not until then can you turn towards another aesthetic, an exploration of a new style. Picasso is a good example of this process. He created seven or eight new styles in his lifetime, taking about ten years to perfect each phase of his art. Within each phase he repeatedly explored one style. This repetition was very important. Repetition deepens and perfects understanding.

Repetition in Artistic Exploration; Seeking Change in Repetition

I'll use two examples to explain the importance of repetition in artistic exploration. The ancient Greeks had strict standards for figures in their art. This aesthetic standard, the beauty of the form, was their style. If they had not had this standard, what kind of situation would we discover? In their sculptures we would see fat people, skinny people, square-faced people, round-faced people; we would see every type of person, just like looking at real life. After you had looked at these works, you would soon forget them, because they lacked a complete singular flavor. In all the works that we see from Ancient Greece, we can find a unified aesthetic. They had pure aesthetic requirements; the head and body proportions adhere to a unified standard. This is repetition. This is seeking change in repetition. This type of repetition strengthens your impression. You look at one piece, you can't remember it. Look at another piece and see the similarities and differences, where there are changes and repetitions, and you say to yourself 'O.K., this is Greek'. You then look at the third piece, the fourth piece, and more and more, and you begin to form in your mind a strong idea of the Greek aesthetic and style. If you see something which is completely different, you can't

remember it; you can't form a complete idea of the artistic system, of the style. I feel that repetition of a form or an aesthetic is very important, because it is a very strong symbol.

In the Russian film *Number Forty-One*, the director understood the power of repetition. His method was to continually repeat the image of the main character's sea-blue eyes. This repeated imagery gives one a very strong impression. The first time you see these eyes, you have no reaction. The second time you begin to have some impression. The third time you begin to feel a little emotion. The fourth time you feel quite moved, and by the fifth time you see them, you understand why every possible event takes place.

Why is it that you can recognize an artist's work? It is because his style is repeated, and in this way has formed a certain "look." In repetition, however, there is change. If ten paintings are exactly the same, you're done for as an artist. At the same time, if today you paint one way and tomorrow you paint another way, you're also finished. You have to repeat the aesthetic, but change the expression. If you work for an entire lifetime, repeating yourself without change, then you have no talent. Picasso was a genius who could change every ten years. If you can change once every twenty years, then you're a Buddha; you have succeeded.

There are would-be artists with great form and color who submit their works to galleries, but their paintings are not distinguishable by style. To be successful you must develop a consistent style, then take your works to the gallery. It is important to persist for a period and perfect your style. If you persist for a lifetime, however, this also will not do.

One Chinese painter who recently held an exhibit of his works in Paris received this comment from an art critic: "The artist's forty years' worth of work seems like it was done in a day. There is no happiness, no anger, no sorrow or joy." This is tragic criticism; forty years of life as an artist appeared as only one day. I give this example in order that you can understand that when I talk of repetition, I don't mean to repeatedly copy one work. There must

be change in each new piece. But it is nonetheless very important to foster repetition of your own individual style. The beauty in repetition will form the power of your style. This is what I have discovered from my own experiences in the study of art.

—*Compiled by Julia Yu & Yiping You*

Illustrations

1 Ting Chün-sheng and Lee Hsiang-chü and their five children **Xian 1943**

2 Ting Shao Kuang, front left, with his older brothers Shaozeng and Shaoyuan, elder sister Shaoxia, younger sister Shaoyun, and younger brother Shaoxiong **1945**

3 Ting Shao Kuang and Liu Bingjiang **Dian Pond, Kunming 1965**

4a Zhang Guangyu
Zhaoshutun hides Nanmarouna's peacock cloak **c. 1950**

4b Zhang Guangyu
Nanmarouna escapes execution **c. 1950**

4c Zhang Guangyu The hermit Palaxi gives
Nanmarouna's bracelet to Zhaoshutun **c. 1950**

4d **Zhang Guangyu** Zhaoshutun and his monkey guide cross the seething Nanmiangaligakang River on the back of a giant black snake **c. 1950**

4e **Zhang Guangyu** Zhaoshutun travels to Mengwodongban in the hollow of the giant man-eating bird's feather **c. 1950**

4f **Zhang Guangyu** Nanmarouna's maid pours over her the bucket of water with the bracelet Zhaoshutun placed in it **c. 1950**

5 **Ting Shao Kuang** Baimiao paintings of Xishuangbanna, detail **1979**

6 **Pan Xunqin** Mount Lu, watercolor **1947**

7 Zhang Ding and Picasso in Paris **1958**

8 **Zhang Ding** An Ancient Tower in Suzhou **1950s**

9 **Zhang Ding** Sunrise at Xiyu Mountain **1984**

10 **Zhang Ding** Ancestral Home of the Mountain Spirit **1987**

11 **Ting Shao Kuang** in front of the Beijing Library, shortly after graduation from the Central Academy of Arts and Crafts

12 **Ting Shao Kuang** (kneeling center) and soldier-peasant-worker students on a field trip to Shilin (The Stone Forest) near Kunming **1972**

13 **Ting Shao Kuang** Liushahe (Running Sand River) **1979**

14 **Some of the Shen She artists** outside the Yunnan Museum
From left to right: Pei Wenkun, Yao Zhonghua, Jiang Tiefeng,
Wang Ruizhang (hidden), He Neng, Dong Xihan, Liu Shaohui, He
Deguang, Ting Shao Kuang, Wang Jingyuan, Chen Zhichuan
Kunming, 1979

15 **Monkey logo**
designed by Jiang Tiefeng, on
Shen She: First Exhibition brochure
July, 1980

16 **Dong Xihan** Untitled
from the Shen She exhibition **1980**

17 **He Deguang**
Early Morning of the Water-Splashing Festival
from the Shen She exhibition **1980**

18 **Sun Jingbo** Repose
from the Shen She exhibition
1980

19 **Chen Zhichuan** June Snow
from the Shen She exhibition
1980

20 **Jiang Tiefeng** Ashima
from the Shen She exhibition **1980**

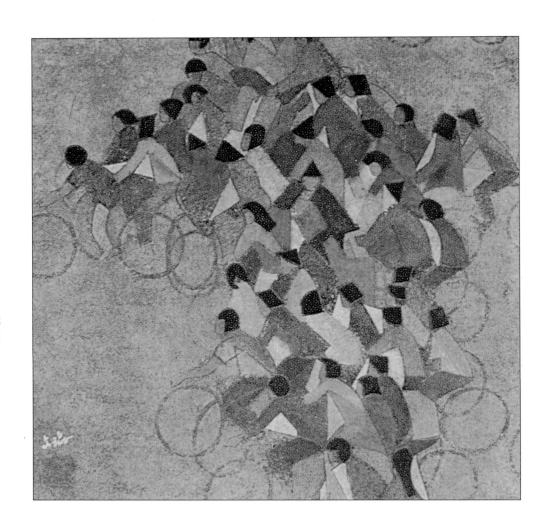

21 **Pei Wenkun** Morning Bicycle Ride
from the Shen She exhibition **1980**

22 **Pei Wenkun** Clear Sky
from the Shen She exhibition **1980**

23 **He Neng** Day Off
from the Shen She exhibition
1980

24 **He Deguang** Golden River
from the Shen She exhibition
1980

25 **Yao Zhonghua** Spirit of the Bull
from the Shen She exhibition **1980**

26 **Liu Shaohui** The Lute Player
from the Shen She exhibition **1980**

27 Yuan Yunsheng
Water-Sprinkling Festival: In Praise of Life
 acrylic on canvas in plaster

28 **Zhu Danian**   Song of the Forest
ceramic tile with enamel overglaze

29 **Ting Shao Kuang** Beauty, Richness, Mystery **1979**

(Bamboo pen and Chinese ink on paper)

30 **Ting Shao Kuang** Tropical Rain Forest **1979**

31 **Ting Shao Kuang** Dai Houses **1979**

32 **Ting Shao Kuang**
Dai Houses in the Jungle **1979**

33 **Ting Shao Kuang** Wa Girl **1979**

34 **Ting Shao Kuang** Hani Girl **1979**

35 **Ting Shao Kuang** Dai Girl **1979**

36 **Ting Shao Kuang** Meili, shenqi de Xishuangbanna (Beautiful, Mysterious Xishuangbanna) **1980**

37 **Ting Shao Kuang** Meili, shenqi de Xishuangbanna
(Beautiful, Mysterious Xishuangbanna) det. **1980**

38　**Jiang Tiefeng**　Shilin (Stone Forest) **1980**

39 **Yao Zhonghua** Jinshajiang (Golden Sand River) **1980**

40 **Liu Bingjiang and Zhou Ling** The Joys of Creation and Harvest **1982**

41 **Ting Shao Kuang** Cradle Song **1984**

42 **Ting Shao Kuang** Twins **1987**

43 **Ting Shao Kuang** Motherhood **1987**

44 **Ting Shao Kuang** Morning Walk **1993**

45 **Ting Shao Kuang** Moonlight **1994**

46 **Ting Shao Kuang** Blue Diamond **1988**

47 **Ting Shao Kuang** Bali Princess I **1994**

48 **Ting Shao Kuang** Han Palace Light **1988**

49 **Ting Shao Kuang** June Bride **1988**

50 **Ting Shao Kuang** The Peacock Princess **1989**

51 **Ting Shao Kuang** Ashima at Sunrise **1985**

52 **Ting Shao Kuang** Moonlight **1988**

53 **Ting Shao Kuang** Night Rider **1987**

54 **Ting Shao Kuang** The Warrior **1986**

55 **Ting Shao Kuang** Ten Suns **1987**

56 **Ting Shao Kuang** Eyes of Prey **1990**

57 **Ting Shao Kuang** Phoenix **1991**

58 **Ting Shao Kuang** Warrior of Thought **1987**

59 **Ting Shao Kuang** The Hunters **1987**

60 **Ting Shao Kuang** Golden Sand River (Jinshajiang) **1987**

65 **Ting Shao Kuang** The Banyan Tree in Moonlight **1989**

66 **Ting Shao Kuang** Under the Beiye Tree **1994**

67 **Ting Shao Kuang** Harmony **1986**

68 **Ting Shao Kuang** Pastoral **1981**

69 **Ting Shao Kuang** Xishuangbanna **1985**

70 **Ting Shao Kuang** Wings of Victory **1984**

71 **Ting Shao Kuang** Wishing for Peace **1988**

72 **Ting Shao Kuang** Purple Dreams **1989**

73 **Ting Shao Kuang** Relaxation **1985**

74 **Ting Shao Kuang** Stone Garden **1986**

75 **Ting Shao Kuang** Life Cycles **1986**

76 **Ting Shao Kuang** Dunhuang Mural **1988**

77 **Ting Shao Kuang** Silk Road **1986**

78 **Ting Shao Kuang** Flowers of Paradise **1992**

79 **Ting Shao Kuang** Orchids and Irises **1993**

80 **Ting Shao Kuang** Bountiful Harvest **1994**

81 **Ting Shao Kuang** Running Sand River **1990**

82 **Ting Shao Kuang** Running Sand River **1990**

83 **Ting Shao Kuang** Sacred Village **1992**

84 **Ting Shao Kuang** Chinese New Year **1994**

85 **Ting Shao Kuang** White Night **1991**

86 **Ting Shao Kuang** Peace and Friendship **1997**

87 **Ting Shao Kuang** Light for Human Rights **1993**

88 **Ting Shao Kuang** Peace, Equality and Development **1995**

89 **Ting Shao Kuang** Religion and Peace **1995**

90 **Ting Shao Kuang** Freedom and Happiness **1995**

91 **Ting Shao Kuang** Culture and Education **1995**

92 **Ting Shao Kuang** Lullaby **1995**

93 **Ting Shao Kuang** Xishuangbanna, detail **1985**

Fourth World Conference on Women
Quatrième Conférence mondiale
sur les femmes
Vierte Weltfrauenkonferenz

FIRST DAY COVER OF THE
UNITED NATIONS POSTAL ADMINISTRATION

94 Set of six stamps commisioned by the United Nations Postal Administration **1995**

Appendix

TITLES OF PAINTINGS IN THE FIRST SHEN SHE EXHIBITION

Ting Shao Kuang
Baimiao Scenery

Wang Jingyuan
(Chinese brush and ink)
Early Spring at the Border
Herding in the Highland
Chengdu and Kunming in Summer
Autumn Colors at Jinsha
Light Rain is Falling
Fragrant Grass in a Remote Spot
Outing
Morning Dew
New Talent
Deep in the Forest

Wang Ruizhang
(Chinese brush and ink)
Bullfight
Morning Mist on the Mountains
Morning Dew
Facing the Sun
Swimming Fish

Wang Tianren
(Oil)
Morning
Clouds over Ehai Lake Darken Chang Mountain
Morning Sun over Ehai Lake
Dai Girl
Tide
Yunnan Scenery (two woodcuts)

Liu Shaohui
(Gouache and ink)
Zhaoshutun series 1: Fight
Zhaoshutun series 2: Love
Longing
Sunset
The Dai Household
Iron Mask
The Lute Player
Folk Story Illustrations
If you have known each other long, don't be suspicious.
I will marry you!
From now on you will have peace!
Regret and Hatred

Zhu Weiming
Hu Lu Xin: Nine lithographs

Sun Jingbo
Repose *(oil)*
Flowers and Birds *(gouache and ink)*

He Neng
(gouache and ink)
Impressions of a Border Village
Camellia
Iris
Little Xing Xing
White Peacock
Day Off

He Deguang
(gouache and ink)
Early Morning of the Water-Splashing Festival
Golden Colors on the Ruili River
Flower Vendor
Wooden-headed Boss *(gouache)*
"The road to redressing wrongs is slow." (Qu Yuan)
Spring Is Here

Li Xiu
Four woodcuts illustrating The Whole Earth Trembles
Child's Play *(gouache and ink)*

Chen Zhichuan
(gouache and ink)
Nature
June Snow
Poppy
Stringed Instrument
Dancing Candlelight
Water

Xiao Jiahe
(Drawings)
Drawing Number One
Drawing Number Two
Drawing Number Three
Refugee
Grandmother

Meng Xueguang

(oil)

Pasture Scene

Sunset in Mountain Village *(gouache)*

Dai Girl

Scenery

Golden Colors of Wumeng

Yao Zhonghua

(oil)

Record of Spring: 1976

Xishuangbanna Pictures

In the Peacock's Village

Silent Killing

Rain at the Qingming Festival

"Spring wind blows new life." *(gouache and ink)*

Spirit of the Bull

Dongchuan Market

Landscape

Interpretation of Michelangelo's Poetry and Painting

Ke De'en

(Chinese brush and ink)

Lu Ban

Hope

Longing

Rest

Mountain Wind

Feeding Chickens

Drawing Water

Princess Wencheng

Lang Sen

Clear Dew *(Chinese brush and ink)*

Dong Xihan

(gouache and ink)

Untitled One

Untitled Two

Scenery

Scenery

Scenery

Jia Guozhong

(gouache and ink)

Opera Mask

Cloth Tiger

Xishuangbanna Feelings

Net

Valley

Green Palace: Six Illustrations

Yuan Ruixin

(gouache and ink)

Boat People

Cormorant

Li Huiniang *(oil)*

Black Woman

Lotus

Penguin

Flowers

Jiang Tiefeng

(gouache and ink)

Monkeys at Play

Chicken

Autumn

Flowers

Love

Bleating Sheep

Noon

Secret of the Sea

Dove

Thumb Girl

Pei Wenkun

(gouache and ink)

Waking Up

Wish

Clear Day

Boats

Fish

Watermelon

Morning Bicycle Ride

Gentle Wind

Morning Make-up

The Composer Xian Xinghai

Liao Ying

Rest *(gouache)*

Green Heat *(oil)*

Li Kaiming

(oil)

Life Sketch of Dehong One

Life Sketch of Dehong Two

LIST OF ILLUSTRATIONS

1. Ting Chün-sheng and Lee Hsiang-chü and their five children, Xian, 1943.

2. Ting Shao Kuang, front left, with his older brothers Shaozeng and Shaoyuan, elder sister Shaoxia, younger sister Shaoyun, and younger brother Shaoxiong, 1945.

3. Ting Shao Kuang and Liu Bingjiang, Dian Pond, Kunming, 1965.

4. **Zhang Guangyu,** Illustrations for *The Peacock Maiden,* early 1950s, reprinted from *Zhang Guang Yu Chatuji,* Beijing: People's Art Press, 1962.

    a. Zhaoshutun hides Nanmarouna's peacock cloak.

    b. Nanmarouna escapes execution.

    c. The hermit Palaxi gives Nanmarouna's bracelet to Zhaoshutun.

    d. Zhaoshutun and his monkey guide cross the seething Nanmiangaligakang River on the back of a giant black snake.

    e. Zhaoshutun travels to Mengwodongban in the hollow of the giant man-eating bird's feather.

    f. Nanmarouna's maid pours over her the bucket of water with the bracelet Zhaoshutun placed in it.

5. **Ting Shao Kuang,** Baimiao paintings of Xishuangbanna, Yunnan People's Publishing House, 1979, detail.

6. **Pang Xunqin, MOUNT LU,** 1947, watercolor, 41x44 cm., reproduced from *Pang Xunqin Huaji,* Beijing: People's Art Press, ca. 1984.

7. Zhang Ding and Picasso in Paris, 1958.

8. **Zhang Ding, AN ANCIENT TOWER IN SUZHOU,** 1950s, ink on paper, artist's collection.

9. **Zhang Ding, SUNRISE AT XIYU MOUNTAIN,** 1984, Great Wall Hotel, Beijing.

10. **Zhang Ding, ANCESTRAL HOME OF THE MOUNTAIN SPIRIT,** 1987, ink on paper, artist's collection.

11. Ting Shao Kuang in front of the Beijing Library, shortly after graduation from the Central Academy of Arts and Crafts.

12. Ting Shao Kuang (kneeling, center) and soldier-peasant-worker students on a field trip to Shilin (The Stone Forest) near Kunming, 1972.

13. **Ting Shao Kuang, LIUSHAHE** (Running Sand River), 1979, bamboo pen and Chinese ink on paper, approximately 24" x 36".

14. Some of the Shen She artists outside the Yunnan Museum, Kunming, 1979. From left to right: Pei Wenkun, Yao Zhonghua, Jiang Tiefeng, Wang Ruizhang (hidden), He Neng, Dong Xihan, Liu Shaohui, He Deguang, Ting Shao Kuang, Wang Jingyuan, Chen Zhichuan.

15. Monkey logo, designed by Jiang Tiefeng, on Shen She: First Exhibition brochure, July, 1980.

16. **Dong Xihan, UNTITLED,** gouache and ink, from the 1980 Shen She exhibition, reprinted from *Meishu congkan* 14 (May 1981), 72.

17. **He Deguang, EARLY MORNING OF THE WATER-SPLASHING FESTIVAL,** gouache and ink, from the 1980 Shen She exhibition, reprinted from *Meishu congkan* 14 (May 1981), 71.

18. **Sun Jingbo, REPOSE,** oil, from the 1980 Shen She exhibition, reprinted from *Meishu congkan* 14 (May 1981), 73.

19. **Chen Zhichuan, JUNE SNOW,** gouache and ink, from the 1980 Shen She exhibition, reprinted from *Meishu congkan* (May 1981), 72.

20. **Jiang Tiefeng, ASHIMA,** gouache and ink, from the 1980 Shen She exhibition, reprinted from *Meishu congkan* (May 1981), 75.

21. **Pei Wenkun, MORNING BICYCLE RIDE,** gouache and ink, from the 1980 Shen She exhibition, reprinted from *Meishu congkan* 14 (May 1981), 72.

22. **Pei Wenkun, CLEAR DAY,** gouache and ink, from the 1980 Shen She exhibition, reprinted from *Meishu yanjiu* 1 (1981), 43.

23. **He Neng, DAY OFF,** oil, from the 1980 Shen She exhibition, reprinted from *Meishu yanjiu* 1 (1981), 43.

24. **He Deguang, GOLDEN RIVER** (Jinshajiang), oil, from the 1980 Shen She exhibition, reprinted from *Meishu congkan* 14 (May 1981), 29.

25. **Yao Zhonghua, SPIRIT OF THE BULL,** gouache and ink, from the 1980 Shen She exhibition, reprinted from *Meishu congkan* 14 (May 1981), 71.

26. **Liu Shaohui, THE LUTE PLAYER,** gouache and ink, from the 1980 Shen She exhibition, reprinted from *Meishu congkan* 14 (May 1981), 70.

27. **Yuan Yunsheng, WATER-SPRINKLING FESTIVAL: IN PRAISE OF LIFE,** acrylic on canvas in plaster, 340 x 2700 cm., reprinted with permission from Joan Lebold Cohen, *The New Chinese Painting,* 1949–1986, New York: Harry N. Abrams, 1987, fig. 33.

28. **Zhu Danian, SONG OF THE FOREST,** ceramic tile with enamel overglaze, 340 x 2000 cm., reprinted with permission from Joan Lebold Cohen, *The New Chinese Painting*, 1949-1986, New York: Harry N. Abrams, 1987, fig. 24.

29. **Ting Shao Kuang, BEAUTY, RICHNESS AND MYSTERY,** 1979, bamboo pen and Chinese ink on paper.

30. **Ting Shao Kuang, TROPICAL RAIN FOREST,** 1979, bamboo pen and Chinese ink on paper.

31. **Ting Shao Kuang, DAI HOUSES,** 1979, bamboo pen and Chinese ink on paper.

32. **Ting Shao Kuang, DAI HOUSES IN THE JUNGLE,** 1979, bamboo pen and Chinese ink on paper.

33. **Ting Shao Kuang, WA GIRL,** 1979, bamboo pen and Chinese ink on paper.

34. **Ting Shao Kuang, HANI GIRL,** 1979, bamboo pen and Chinese ink on paper.

35. **Ting Shao Kuang, DAI GIRL,** 1979, bamboo pen and Chinese ink on paper.

36. **Ting Shao Kuang, MEILI, SHENQI DE XISHUANGBANNA** (Beautiful, Mysterious Xishuangbanna), 1980, acrylic, gouache, and mineral pigment on silk, Great Hall of the People, Beijing.

37. **Ting Shao Kuang,** detail of **BEAUTIFUL, MYSTERIOUS XISHUANGBANNA,** 1980, acrylic, gouache, and mineral pigment on silk, Great Hall of the People, Beijing.

38. **Jiang Tiefeng, SHILIN** (Stone Forest), 1980, acrylic, gouache, and mineral pigment on silk, Great Hall of the People, Beijing.

39. **Yao Zhonghua, JINSHAJIANG** (Golden Sands River), 1980, oil on canvas, Great Hall of the People, Beijing.

40. **Liu Bingjiang and Zhou Ling, THE JOYS OF CREATION AND HARVEST,** 1982, acrylic on canvas in plaster, Beijing Hotel.

41. **Ting Shao Kuang, CRADLE SONG,** 1984, mineral pigment, Chinese ink and gouache on paper, 41" x 41".

42. **Ting Shao Kuang, TWINS,** 1987, mineral pigment, Chinese ink and gouache on paper, 88" x 40".

43. **Ting Shao Kuang, MOTHERHOOD,** 1987, mineral pigment, Chinese ink and gouache on paper, 40" x 41".

44. **Ting Shao Kuang, MORNING WALK,** 1993, mineral pigment, Chinese ink and gouache on paper.

45. **Ting Shao Kuang, MOONLIGHT,** 1994, mineral pigment, Chinese ink and gouache on paper.

46. **Ting Shao Kuang, BLUE DIAMOND,** 1988, mineral pigment, Chinese ink and gouache on paper, 41" x 41".

47. **Ting Shao Kuang, BALI PRINCESS I,** 1994, mineral pigment, Chinese ink and gouache on paper.

48. **Ting Shao Kuang, HAN PALACE LIGHT,** 1988, mineral pigment, Chinese ink and gouache on paper, 41" x 41".

49. **Ting Shao Kuang, JUNE BRIDE,** 1988, mineral pigment, Chinese ink and gouache on paper, 41" x 40".

50. **Ting Shao Kuang, THE PEACOCK PRINCESS,** 1989, mineral pigment, Chinese ink and gouache on paper, 40" x 40".

51. **Ting Shao Kuang, ASHIMA AT SUNRISE,** 1985, mineral pigment, Chinese ink and gouache on paper, 40" x 41".

52. **Ting Shao Kuang, MOONLIGHT,** 1988, mineral pigment, Chinese ink and gouache on paper, 41" x 42".

53. **Ting Shao Kuang, NIGHT RIDER,** 1987, mineral pigment, Chinese ink and gouache on paper, 41.5" x 31".

54. **Ting Shao Kuang, THE WARRIOR,** 1986, mineral pigment, Chinese ink and gouache on paper, 40" x 41".

55. **Ting Shao Kuang, TEN SUNS,** 1987, mineral pigment, Chinese ink and gouache on paper, 41" x 40".

56. **Ting Shao Kuang, EYES OF PREY,** 1990, mineral pigment, Chinese ink and gouache on paper, 40" x 40".

57. **Ting Shao Kuang, PHOENIX,** 1991, mineral pigment, Chinese ink and gouache on paper.

58. **Ting Shao Kuang, WARRIOR OF THOUGHT,** 1987, mineral pigment, Chinese ink and gouache on paper, 40" x 40".

59. **Ting Shao Kuang, THE HUNTERS,** 1987, mineral pigment, Chinese ink and gouache on paper, 40" x 41".

60. **Ting Shao Kuang, GOLDEN SAND RIVER** (Jinshajiang), 1987, mineral pigment, Chinese ink and gouache on paper, 40" x 41".

61. **Ting Shao Kuang, THE SOUND OF ROARING BILLOWS,** 1986, mineral pigment, Chinese ink and gouache on paper, 40" x 40".

62. **Ting Shao Kuang, DISTANT DREAMS,** 1987, mineral pigment, Chinese ink and gouache on paper, 40" x 41".

63. **Ting Shao Kuang, MERMAIDS,** 1986, mineral pigment, Chinese ink and gouache on paper, 40" x 41".

64. **Ting Shao Kuang, FLOATING MARKET,** 1989, mineral pigment, Chinese ink and gouache on paper, 40"x 40".

65. **Ting Shao Kuang, THE BANYAN TREE IN MOONLIGHT,** 1989, mineral pigment, Chinese ink and gouache on paper, 41.5" x 40".

66. **Ting Shao Kuang, UNDER THE BEIYE TREE** (Dance of the Peacock), 1994, mineral pigment, Chinese ink and gouache on paper, 104 x 104 cm.

67. **Ting Shao Kuang, HARMONY,** 1986, mineral pigment, Chinese ink and gouache on paper, 30" x 30".

FOOTNOTES

[1]Other children of Ting Chün-sheng and Lee Hsiang-chü are Ding Shaozeng (male, 1931), Ding Shaoyuan (male, 1933), Ding Xiaoxia (female, 1936), Ding Xiaoyun (female, 1942), Ding Shaoxiong (male, 1945) and Ding Shaocheng (male, 1952). I have used *pinyin* romanization throughout the text except for Ting Shao Kuang's name and the names of his parents. The modified Wade-Giles spelling of Ting Shao Kuang's name is the one he uses professionally. As his parents were prominent Taiwanese citizens, I have chosen also to retain the Wade-Giles spelling of their names, with the alternate *pinyin* romanization given in brackets.

[2]*Jianchayuan Ding gu weiyuan Junsheng shishi zhounian ji-nian ji (Commemoration of the Anniversary of the Death of Investigative Officer Ding Junsheng),* Taipei, 1980.

[3]Interview with Liu Binjiang, Beijing, June 1990.

[4]*Zhongyang Meishu Xueyuan Fushu Zhongxue.*

[5]Interview with Ting Shao Kuang, Los Angeles, January 1991.

[6]"Exhibition of Mexican Graphic Art," *Chinese Literature, 3* (March 1956), 209-210.

[7]"Picasso in Peking," *People's China* (January 1, 1957), 41.

[8]"Tunhuang Art Treasures," *Chinese Literature 3* (March 1956), 210-11.

[9]Interview with Zhang Shiyan, Los Angeles, January 1991.

[10]Jack London, writing in the late nineteenth century, was one of the few American writers whose works were translated almost immediately into Russian. His anti-capitalist ideas, embedded in novels written especially for boys, were also widely read in Chinese translation. The novel *Jean Christophe,* by Romain Rolland (1866-1944) (translated into English ca. 1913 by Gilbert Cannan) was influential among socialists in various parts of the world in the first part of the twentieth century, including the United States in the 1910s.

[11]Interview with Ting Shao Kuang, Oxford, Ohio, September 1990.

[12]Ibid.

[13]Ibid.

[14]Born 1885. Founded Shanghai Art Academy with Liu Haisu in 1912. See Michael Sullivan, *Chinese Art in the Twentieth Century,* London: Faber and Faber, 1959, pp. 47-8, 88.

[15]*Zhang Guang Yu Chatuji,* preface by Zhang Ding. Beijing: People's Art Press, second edition, 1980. [First edition 1962]

[16]Sullivan, p. 65.

[17]Interview with Zhong Shuheng and Liu Jude, Beijing, June, 1990. Zhong Shuheng remembers seeing the movie as a child. She said, "The movie made a big wave in Chinese art circles. Everyone saw the movie. I was very young, but I watched the film and felt touched. That's how I knew there was a Zhang Guangyu."

[18]Interview with Ting Shao Kuang, Oxford, Ohio, September 1990. In an unpublished paper, "The Chinese Writers of the New Culture Movement and the New Village Movement in Taisho Japan," Fujiya Kawashima traces Mao Zedong's ideas about art and literature to the influence of the New Culture Movement.

[19]Interview with Ting Shao Kuang, Oxford, Ohio, September 1990.

[20]For a translation of the story into English see *Folktales from China,* Beijing: Foreign Languages Press, third edition, 1981; or, "The Peacock Maiden," *Chinese Literature 4* (April, 1958), 80-95.

[21]Interview with Yuan Yunyi in Beijing, June 1990. Yuan Yunyi is also fond of pointing out that her husband has three famous students—Zhao Wuji in Paris, Ting Shao Kuang in the United States, and Wu Guanzhong in China. She notes her late husband's friendship with the Sinologist Joseph Levenson, art historian Michael Sullivan, and the artist Modigliani with pride. Pang Xunqin has a number of relatives who are painters, including a daughter, Pang Tao, who with her husband, Lin Gang, teaches painting at the Central Academy of Fine Arts. In 1990, a nine-member Pang family exhibition was held in Taipei. A memorial hall has just been built for Pang Xunqin in Jiangsu; Ting Shao Kuang's $20,000 contribution facilitated its completion.

[22]See Ellen J. Laing, *The Winking Owl: Art in the People's Republic of China,* Berkeley: University of California Press, 1988, pp. 28-29.

[23]Sullivan, 1959, pp. 51-52.

[24]Sullivan, 1959, pp. 52-53.

[25]Sullivan, 1959, pp. 55-56.

[26]Six examples of his works, plus a photograph of him taken in Chengdu in 1944, are included in Sullivan, *Chinese Art of the Twentieth Century.* Five more paintings have been published in Mayching Kao, ed., *Twentieth-Century Chinese Painting,* Oxford: Oxford University Press, 1988, pp. 156-160.

[27]An album of landscapes painted in the 1940s and flower still lifes painted in the 1960s and 1970s was published in Beijing by People's Art Press in 1984.

[28]Their rivalry began in Paris in the 1920s at which time Xu Beihong was a proponent of French academic art, Pang Xunqin and Liu Haisu favored the newer movements of impressionism, cubism, and fauvism. Xu Beihong's distaste for modern art led him to remark that the Chinese characters for Matisse—*ma ti si*—should be changed to the homophones "horse-kick-dead" or "kick the horse to death." This was not only a jibe aimed at Matisse, but probably also a malicious reference to the exhibitions of art held annually in Shanghai between 1919 and 1927 by Liu Haisu and his students called the Heavenly Horse Art Festival *(Tianma Huahui).*

[29]Minneapolis: Fingerhut Group Publishers, 1988, p. 104.

[30]Interview with Zhang Ding, Beijing, June 1990.

[31]For a biographical sketch of Zhang Ding see Joan Lebold Cohen, *The New Chinese Painting: 1949–1986,* New York: Harry N. Abrams, 1987, pp. 28-33.

[32]Interview with Zhang Ding, Beijing, June 1990.

[33]For a brief biographical sketch of Yuan Yunfu see Joan Lebold Cohen, *The New Chinese Painting: 1949–1986,* New York: Harry N. Abrams, 1987, pp. 34-36.

[34]Interview with Yuan Yunsheng in Beijing, June, 1990.

[35]Ibid.

[36]Interview with Ting Shao Kuang, Oxford, Ohio, September 1990.

[37]Ibid.

[38]Ibid.

[39]Ting Shao Kuang left these paintings with his teacher, and they were subsequently lost. Ting remembers this series of ink landscapes on paper as being more spontaneous and relaxed than his later meticulous *baimiao* works.

[40]The normal length of time for student field study was from one to three months. Ting Shao Kuang had already taken one trip to the Yellow River, using up his travel allowance. This second trip was sponsored by Zhang Guangyu.

[41]As a Rightist, Pang Xunqin was not allowed to vote.

[42]Ellen Johnston Laing, "Art between 1960 and 1965; Part One: Between 1960 and 1962," *The Winking Owl: Art in the People's Republic of China,* Berkeley: University of California Press, 1988, pp. 33-39.

[43]Zhang Ding remembers his failure to keep two favorite students, Ting Shao Kuang and Lian Weiyun, in Beijing as a reflection of the waning of his political power. (Interview with Zhang Ding, Beijing, June 1990.)

[44]Interview with He Deguang, Los Angeles, January 1991.

[45]Ibid.

[46]Interview with Zhou Ling, Chicago, November 1990.

[47]There were three classes of bad families; Jiang Tiefeng belonged to the worst. In decreasing order, they were 1) those whose parents had committed capital crimes; 2) those whose parents had been imprisoned; and 3) those whose parents had the wrong political backgrounds, such as Kuomintang sympathizers, Rightists, or intellectuals.

[48]The Four Cleanups was part of the Socialist Education Campaign that was to help peasants better organize the collective farms and teach them socialist doctrines. For a more complete discussion of this movement, see Jonathan D. Spence, *The Search for Modern China,* New York: W. W. Norton, 1990, pp. 590-596.

[49]Interview with Ting Shao Kuang, Oxford, Ohio, September 1990.

[50]The Yunnan Art Institute was restored in 1980.

[51]The four bad elements were *di, fu, fan, huai:* landlords *(dizhu),* rich peasants *(funong),* counterrevolutionaries *(fangeming),* and bad elements *(huaifenzi).* Ting Shao Kuang was classified as a counterrevolutionary.

[52]Interview with Ting Shao Kuang, Oxford, Ohio, September 1990.

[53]The youthful Red Guards were encouraged to travel throughout China for a short period during the Cultural Revolution and were allowed free passage on China's railways.

[54]Ting Shao Kuang published an account of this visit to Maijishan in "*Zhongguo xiandai yishu zai shijie de diwei yu qiantu* (The Position and Future of Modern Chinese Art in the World)," *Guoji ribao* (International Daily News), April 17, 1984.

[55]Interview with Ting Shao Kuang, Oxford, Ohio, September 1990.

[56]Interview with Zhang Ding, Beijing, June 1990.

[57]Ibid.

[58]Ibid.

[59]In Beijing in June 1990 I saw a group of paintings she had done at the age of six. The sense of design and color was beautiful and astonishing for a child that age. Ironically, to save precious paper the paintings were done on the back of a calendar printed in the late 1960s. The calendar prints were red flag-waving scenes done in a monotonous socialist-realist style, while the paintings on the back were fresh, original, and charming. Liu Ye graduated from the Central Academy of Fine Arts in 1993, and works with her mother, Zhou Ling, in Chicago.

[60]Interview with Yao Zhonghua, Kunming, June 1990.

[61]Interview with Ting Shao Kuang, Oxford, Ohio, September 1990.

[62]Lei Feng was a soldier who was known to be always willing to help other people. Everyone in China, especially the children, was admonished to follow the example of Lei Feng.

[63]Interview with Ting Shao Kuang, Oxford, Ohio, September 1990.

[64]Ibid.

[65]Ting Shao Kuang has no photographs of the paintings and doesn't believe they were ever published in Chinese art journals because of his lack of interest in meeting Madame Mao. I have not come across reproductions of them; while my research in Chinese periodicals has been extensive it has not been exhaustive. Ting believes they were published in a Hong Kong art journal, but he has no record of the journal or date. Ting also mentioned that the paintings were used in a movie about Qin Weng for which he has no documentation.

[66]Interview with Ting Shao Kuang, Los Angeles, January 1991.

[67]Ting Shao Kuang and his wife were very poor. They first lived in a ruined one-room village shrine that was assigned to them by Zhang Daxi's song and dance company. Later they moved to a cramped two-room dormitory house that also belonged to the company. Zhang Daxi would stay in the second room with her small daughter, but the house was still filled with cigarette smoke and excited chatter.

[68]Interview with Zhou Ling, Chicago, November 1990.

[69]Ibid.

[70]Interview with Liu Jude and Zhong Shuheng, Beijing, June 1990. Liu Jude and Zhong Shuheng are husband and wife, both currently professors of painting at the Central Academy of Arts and Crafts in Beijing. They have two school-aged sons who live at home and who also paint.

[71]Interview with Liu Jude and Zhong Shuheng, Beijing, June, 1990.

[72]Each artist interviewed had a different memory of exactly who had attended the night meetings in Ting's home. The artist friends met for the decade between 1969 and 1979, so the group naturally varied.

[73]Interview with Zhong Shuheng and Liu Jude, Beijing, June 1990.

[74]Interview with Ting Shao Kuang, Oxford, Ohio, September 1990.

[75]Interview with Tong Jinxia and Luo Wenzhi, Kunming, June 1990.

[76]Interview with Ting Shao Kuang, Oxford, Ohio, September 1990.

[77]The following definitions for the word *shen* are from Liang Shih-chiu, ed., *A New Practical Chinese-English Dictionary.* Taipei: The Far East Book Company, 1971, p. 709.

[78]Interview with Yao Zhonghua, Kunming, June 1990.

[79]Interview with Ting Shao Kuang, Oxford, Ohio, September 1990.

[80]Interview with He Neng, Los Angeles, January 1991.

[81]Zhou Yang, "Chinese Literature and Art: Our Lessons and Tasks Ahead," *Beijing Review* 22:50 (December 14, 1979), 8-15.

[82]From the printed pamphlet *Shen She: First Exhibition,* July 1980. The preface was composed jointly by the officers of Shen She. A list of works in the exhibition was also included in the brochure (see pp. 137-138).

[83]Interview with Yao Zhonghua, Kunming, June 1990.

[84]Zhou Liangpei, "*Huabi xia de zhexue: Kan Kunming Shen She huazhan* (The Philosophy Behind the Brush: A Look at Kunming's Shen She Painting Exhibition)," *Meishu yanjiu 1* (1981), 69-71; color reproductions p. 43. Paintings reproduced are He Neng, *Day Off,* oil; Pei Wenkun, *Clear Day,* gouache and ink (misprinted "oil" in *Meishu yanjiu*); Yao Zhonghua, *Interpretation of Michelangelo's Poetry and Painting,* gouache and ink; Liu Shaohui, *Iron Mask,* gouache and ink; and Chen Zhichuan, *June Snow,* gouache and ink. Sun Jingbo's graduation piece from the CAFA was reproduced in the same issue, pp.44-45.

[85]Liu Shaohui, "*Yishu suiganlu* (My Thoughts on Art)," *Meishu congkan 14* (May 1981), 31-37. Jiang Tiefeng, "*Tan Zhongguohua de chuangxin—shidai, geren* (A Discussion of New Creations in Chinese Painting—The Period and Individuals)," ibid., 11-15. Reproductions of works by Jiang Tiefeng, Jia Guozhong, Chen Zhichuan, Li Xiu, Zhu Weiming, He Neng, Pei Wenkun, Xiao Jiahe, He Deguang, and Wang Jingyuan, pp. 16-30. Color reproductions of works by Liu Shaohui, Yao Zhonghua, He Deguang, Chen Zhichuan, Dong Xihan, Pei Wenkun, Jia Guozhong, Liao Ying, Jiang Tiefeng, and Sun Jingbo, pp. 70-75.

[86]Interview with Zhang Shiyan, Los Angeles, January 1991.

[87]Interview with He Neng, Los Angeles, January 1991.

[88]Shi Ye, "*Yanjiu xingshi guilü; tanqiu huihua yuyan: Ji 'Yunnan Shiren Huazhan' zuotanhui* (Study Principles of Artistic Form; Explore the Language of Painting: A Symposium on the Yunnan Ten-person Painting Exhibition," *Meishu 11* (1981), 61-63.

[89]Joan Cohen has referred to this statement about Jiang Tiefeng's work in two of her publications. It is a story that has been retold many times by artists who were in attendance at the meeting.

[90]Shi Ye.

[91]Interview with Yao Zhonghua, Kunming, June 1991.

[92]Xia Shuoqi, "A Brief Introduction to Five Yunnan Painters," *Chinese Literature* (May 1982), 123.

[93]For example, see the works from Yunnan illustrated in *Chinese Literature* (Autumn 1988), 96 ff.

[94]Interview with Wu Guanzhong, Beijing, June 1990.

[95]See "New Murals at Beijing International Airport," *Chinese Literature* (April 1980), 114 ff. for reproductions of each of the works.

[96]Ting Shao Kuang, *Xishuangbanna baimiao xieshengji* (Album of Life Drawings from Xishuangbanna), Kunming: Yunnan People's Publishing House, August 1979.

[97]Ting took the design with him to the United States, where he sold it to a private collector in Taiwan.

[98]From the editorial, "Enliven the Literature and Art of Minority Nationalities," *Renmin ribao,* October 21, 1980, 1. [Translated into English in Daily Report: PRC Activities (October 31, 1980), L22.] See also, Mongolian Branch of the Chinese Artists' Association, "To Thoroughly Implement the Government Policy to Glorify the Minorities We Should Develop Minority Art," *Meishu* (Dec. 1979), 41-42.

[99]Interview with Gary Lichtenstein, San Francisco, January 1991.

[100]Gary Lichtenstein, "Collaboration as an Art Form," in *Ting Shao Kuang Serigraphs: Catalogue Raisonné,* Woodland Hills: Segal Fine Art, 1991.

[101]Interviews with Ting Shao Kuang, Los Angeles, January 1991, and with Zhong Shuheng, Beijing, June 1990.

[102]See illustrations in "Old Rock Paintings," *Chinese Literature 6* (1966), 127-28.

[103]Interview with Ting Shao Kuang, Los Angeles, January 1991.

[104]Interview with Ting Shao Kuang, Oxford, Ohio, September 1991.

[105]Ibid.

[106]Interview with Wu Guanzhong, Beijing, June 1990.

GLOSSARY OF CHINESE NAMES

Chen Danqing	陳丹青	Meng Xueguang	孟薛光
Chen Zhichuan	陳之川	Ni Yide	倪眙德
Ding Li	丁 立	Pang Tao	龐 濤
Ding Shaocheng	丁紹成	Pang Xunqin	龐熏琹
Ding Shaoyuan	丁紹元	Pei Wenkun	裴文琨
Ding Xiaoyun	丁曉雲	Qi Baishi	齊白石
Ding Xiaoxia	丁曉霞	Qin Yuanyue	秦元閱
Ding Shaoxiong	丁紹雄	Quan Zhenghuan	權正環
Ding Shaozeng	丁紹曾	Shen She	申 社
Ding Ting	丁 婷	Sun Jingbo	孫景波
Dong Qichang	董 婷	Ting Chün-sheng	丁俊生
Dong Xihan	董錫漢	Ting Shao Kuang	丁紹光
Dong Xiwen	董希文	Wang Jingyuan	王競元
Gu Kaizhi	顧愷之	Wang Ruizhang	王瑞章
Guan Shanyue	關山月	Wang Tianren	王天任
He Deguang	何德光	Wu Guanzhong	吳冠中
He Neng	何 能	Wu Zuoren	吳作人
Hua Junwu	華君武	Xiao Huixiang	蕭惠祥
Huang Yongyu	黃永玉	Xiao Jiahe	肖嘉禾
Jiang Feng	江 豐	Xie He	謝 赫
Jiang Tiefeng	蔣鐵鋒	Xishuangbanna	西雙版納
Ke De'en	柯德恩	Xu Beihong	徐悲鴻
Lang Sen	郎 森	Xu Yansun	徐燕蓀
Lee Hsiang-chün Ting	丁李湘君	Yao Zhonghua	姚鐘華
Li Huaji	李化吉	Yuan Ruixin	袁瑞新
Li Kaiming	李開明	Yuan Yunfu	袁運甫
Li Keran	李可染	Yuan Yunsheng	袁運生
Li Xiu	李 秀	Zhao Wuji	趙無極
Liang Kai	梁 楷	Zhang Daqian	張大千
Lin Fengmian	林風眠	Zhang Daxi	張達喜
Lin Gang	林 崗	Zhang Ding	張 仃
Liao Ying	廖 熒	Zhang Guangyu	張光宇
Liu Bingjiang	劉秉江	Zhang Yuguang	張聿光
Liu Haisu	劉海粟	Zhong Shuheng	鐘蜀珩
Liu Jude	劉巨德	Zhou Ling	周 菱
Liu Shaohui	劉紹薈	Zhu Danian	祝大年
Liu Ziming	劉自鳴	Zhu Weiming	朱維明

BIBLIOGRAPHY

Andrews, Julia F.
Painters and Politics in the People's Republic of China, 1949-1979. Berkeley: University of California Press, c1994.

————.
"Traditional Painting in New China: Guohua and the Anti-Rightist Campaign," The Journal of Asian Studies 49:3 (August 1990), 555-585.

Bao Guanren.
"From Beijing to Beverly Hills," Asia, Inc., February 1993, 84-87.

Bao Minglian.
"Ding Shaoguang de Yishu guan he chenggong zhi lu," Yishu shijie (World of Art), Shanghai, April 1992, 4-14.

Ben Kanji.
"Shoudu guoji jichang houjilou bihua luocheng (The Murals in the Waiting Room of the National Airport in the Capital Are Completed)," *Meishu 11* (November, 1979), 3-9.

Chang, Arnold.
Painting in the People's Republic of China: The Politics of Style. Boulder: Westview Press, 1980.

Chang Ding.
"Folk Toys," *Chinese Literature 6* (June 1959), 140-42.

Chang Kwang-Yu.
"There's a Reservoir East of Our Village," *Chinese Literature 4* (April 1960), 6 ff.

"Chuangzhao shouhuo huanle: Liu Binjiang Zhou Ling hezuo de bihua (The Joys of Creation and Harvest: The Mural Painting by Liu Binjiang and Zhou Ling)," *Meishujia* (October 1, 1982), 1; 79-80; cover.

Cohen, Joan Lebold.
Yunnan School: A Renaissance in Chinese Painting. Minneapolis: Fingerhut Group Publishers, 1988.

————.
The New Chinese Painting, 1949-1986. New York: Harry N. Abrams, 1987.

————.
Painting the Chinese Dream: Chinese Art Thirty Years after the Revolution. Northampton: Smith College Museum of Art, 1982.

Cohen, Joan Lebold and Cohen, Jerome Alan.
China Today and Her Ancient Treasures, New York: Harry N. Abrams, 1980.

Contemporary Oil Paintings from the People's Republic of China. Oklahoma City: The Hefner Galleries, 1987.

Croizier, Ralph.
"Art and Society in Modern China, A Review Article," *The Journal of Asian Studies* 49:3 (August 1990), 586-602.

————.
"Chinese Art in the Chiang Ch'ing Era," *The Journal of Asian Studies,* 38 (1979), 303-311.

Deng Qiyao.
"Prints from Yunnan," *Chinese Literature 3* (Autumn 1988), 97-98.

"Deng Xiaoping, Li Xiannian View Paintings at Beijing Airport," *Daily Report: People's Republic of China* (October 15, 1979), L20-21.

"Ding Shaoguang huihua Yishu," Chinese Arts, vol. 12, Beijing, n.d. (1994?), 16-22.

Eberhard, Wolfram.
China's Minorities: Yesterday and Today. Belmont, California: The Wadsworth Civilization in Asia Series, 1982.

"Exhibition of Mexican Graphic Art," *Chinese Literature 3* (March 1956), 209-10.

Gladney, Dru C.
"Representing Nationality in China: Refiguring Major/Minor Identities," *Journal of Asian Studies,* vol. 53, no. 1 (February 1994), 92-123.

Guo Xu, Xu Kun and Miller, Lucien, translators.
"Two Yunnan Tales," *Renditions 31* (Spring 1989), 48-66.

He Erguan.
"Yunnan huapai zai Meiguo (The Yunnan School in the United States)," Xin Xi 6 (n.d., ca. 1990), 15-19.

"He Neng de zhongcaihua (He Neng's Heavy Color Painting)," *Meishujia 24* (Feb. 1, 1982), 11.

Huang Yongyu.
"Yi zhang bihua de duansheng (The Building of a Mural Painting)," *Meishu* (June 1982), 16.

Jianchayuan Ding Gu weiyuan Junsheng shishi zhounian jinian ji (Commemoration of the Anniversary of the Death of Investigative Officer Ting Chün-sheng). Taipei, 1980.

Jiang Tiefeng.
"Tan zhongguohua de chuangxin—shidai, geren (A Discussion of New Creations in Chinese Painting—The Period and Individuals)," *Meishu congkan 14* (May 1981), 11-15.

"Jiang Tiefeng de zhongcaihua (Jiang Tiefeng's Heavy Color Painting)," *Meishujia 24* (Feb. 1, 1982), 10-11.

Kao, Mayching, ed.
Twentieth-Century Chinese Painting, Oxford: Oxford University Press, 1988.

Kawashima, Fujiya.
"The Chinese Writers of the New Culture Movement and the New Village Movement in Taisho Japan," unpublished paper read at the Ohio East Asian Seminar, Columbus, Ohio, June 1, 1991.

Laing, Ellen Johnston.
An Index to Reproductions of Paintings by Twentieth-Century Chinese Artists. Eugene: University of Oregon Asian Studies Program Publication No. 6, 1984.

————.
The Winking Owl: Art in the People's Republic of China. Berkeley: University of California Press, 1988.

Lan Yi.
"The Painter Zhang Ding," *Chinese Literature 4* (April 1983), 49-54 ff.

Li, Chu-tsing.
Trends in Modern Chinese Painting. Ascona: Artibus Asiae, 1979.

Liu Shaohui.
"*Yishu suiganlu* (My Thoughts on Art)," *Meishu congkan 14* (May 1981), 31-37.

————.
"Illustrations for Zhaoshutun," *Meishu* (May 1980), 23.

Macdonnell, Anna Manzoni, and Murobushi, Tetsuro.
The Art of Ting Shao Kuang. Tokyo: Kodansha/Segal Fine Art, 1989.

Meishu (Oct. 1981). Fifteen articles about wall painting accompanied by more than seventy illustrations.

Meishu (Dec. 1982), 26 and back cover. Photographs of the Beijing Hotel mural by Liu Bingjiang and Zhou Ling.

Miller, Lucien.
South of the Clouds: Tales from Yunnan, University of Washington Press, 1994. (A Yunnan landscape painting by Ting Shao Kuang was used for the award-winning jacket cover of this book.)

Mongolian Branch of the Chinese Artists' Association.
"*Guanche dangde minzu zhengce fazhan minzu meishu shiye* (Thoroughly Implement the Party's Policy to Glorify the Minorities; Develop Minority Art)," *Meishu* (Dec. 1979).

"Murals in Beijing International Airport," *Beijing Review* 23:2 (Jan. 14, 1980), 29-30.

New Era in Chinese Painting. Chicago: Signet Fine Art/East West Limited Editions, 1988.

"New Murals at Beijing International Airport," *Chinese Literature 4* (April 1980), 114 ff.

"Old Rock Paintings [in Yunnan Province]," *Chinese Literature 6* (June 1966), 127-28.

Painting from the Heart: Selected Works of Wu Guanzhong. Beijing: Foreign Languages Press, 1990.

"Paintings by Liu Binjiang and Zhou Ling," *Chinese Literature 1* (January 1983), 120 ff.

"Paintings from Yunnan Province," *Chinese Literature 5* (May 1982), 122 ff.; front and back covers.

Pang Xunqin.
Jiushi zheyang zou guolai de [It went exactly that way: an autobiography]. Beijing: *Shenghuo dushu xinzhi sanlian shudian,* 1988.

"The Peacock Maiden," translated by Alex Young, illustrated by Chang Kuang-yu, *Chinese Literature 4* (April 1958), 80-95.

"Picasso in Peking," *People's China* (Jan. 1, 1957), 41.

Selected Paintings of Ting Shao Kuang, with an introduction by Yuan Yunfu. Beijing: Foreign Language Press, 1992.

"*Shen She shoujie huazhan zuopingxuan* (A Selection of Paintings from Shen She: First Exhibition)," *Meishu congkan 14* (May 1981), 70-75.

Shi Ye.
"*Yanjiu xingshi guilü; tanqiu huihua yuyan: Ji 'Yunnan Shiren Huazhan' zuotanhui* (Study Principles of Artistic Form; Explore the Language of Painting: A Symposium on the Yunnan Ten-person Painting Exhibition," *Meishu 11* (1981), 61-63.

Shi Xianrong.
"American Literature in China," *Chinese Literature* (Autumn 1984), 207-12.

Spence, Jonathan D.
The Search for Modern China. New York: W. W. Norton, 1990.

Strassberg, Richard E.
"I Don't Want to Play Cards with Cézanne" and Other Works: Selections from the Chinese "New Wave" and "Avante-garde" Art of the Eighties. Pasadena: Pacific Asia Museum, 1991.

Strassberg, Richard E., and Nielsen, Waldemar A.
Beyond the Open Door: Contemporary Paintings from the People's Republic of China. Pasadena: Pacific Asia Museum, 1987.

Sullivan, Michael.
Chinese Art in the Twentieth Century. London: Faber and Faber, 1959.
————.
Art and Artists of Twentieth Century China. Berkeley: University of California Press, 1996.

Tao Yongbai.
"A New Mural and Its Creators," *Chinese Literature 1* (Jan. 1983), 121-125. [Liu Bingjiang and Zhou Ling]

Ting Shao Kuang.
The World of Ting Shao Kuang. Tokyo: Japan Broadcast Publishing Company (NHK), 1995.
————.
Xishuangbanna baimiao xieshengji (Album of Life Drawings from Xishuangbanna), Kunming: Yunnan People's Publishing House, August, 1979.
————.
"*Zhongguo xiandai yishu zai shijie de diwei yu qiantu* (The Position and Future of Modern Chinese Art in the World)," *Guoji ribao* (International Daily News) (April 17-28), 1984.

Ting Shao Kuang. Chinese Master Painters, volume 20. Taipei: Taiwan Mac Educational Company, 1995.

Ting Shao Kuang. Paris: Galerie Bernheim, June 1990.
"*Ting Shao Kuang,*" *Twenty-first Century Prints,* vol. 2, 1991, Tokyo.

Ting Shao Kuang: Serigraphs (1986-1991); Bronzes (1989-1991). Tokyo: Galleria Prova, 1991.

Ting Shao Kuang. Exhibition Catalog for Galerie Bernheim, Paris. Woodland Hills: Segal Fine Art, 1990.

Ting Shao Kuang. Exhibition Catalog for Hiestand Gallery, Miami University, Oxford, Ohio. Woodland Hills: Segal Fine Art, 1990.

Ting Shao Kuang Serigraphs: Catalogue Raisonné. Woodland Hills: Segal Fine Art, 1991.

"Tunhuang Art Treasures," *Chinese Literature 3* (March 1956), 210-11.

Wicks, Ann Barrott.
Huihua tiantang: Ding Shaoguang de Yishu. Beijing: *Renmin meishu chuban she,* 1992.

Xia Shuoqi.
"A Brief Introduction to Five Yunnan Painters," *Chinese Literature 5* (May 1982), 123-125.

Yao Zhonghua and Zeng Xiaofeng.
"Primitive Folk Art of Yunnan *(Yunnan minjian yuanshi Yishu mantan)*," *Modern Artists,* Sichuan Fine Arts Institute, 3 (1986), 68-75.

Yuan Yunfu.
"*Bihua shijian zhong suo xiangdao de* (My Thoughts While Practicing Wall Painting)," *Meishu 1* (1980), 1-5.
————.
"Reviving Chinese Mural Art," *Chinese Literature 4* (April 1980), 115-20.

Yuan Yunfu Huaji (Works by Yuan Yunfu). Beijing: People's Art Press, 1980.

Yuan Yunsheng.
"*Bihua zhi meng* (Wall Painting Dream)," *Meishu 1* (1980), 5-8.

"Yunnan Graphic Art," *Chinese Literature* (Autumn 1988), 96 ff.

"*Yunnan Shiren Huazhan xuan* (A Selection from the Yunnan Ten-person Painting Exhibition)," *Meishu 11* (1981), 42-43; 45.

Zhang Ding Huaji (Works by Zhang Ding). Beijing: People's Art Press, 1982.

Zhang Guang Yu Chatuji, preface by Zhang Ding. Beijing: People's Art Press, 1962, second edition 1980.

Zhi Bian.
"The Beijing Art Exhibition," *Chinese Literature 2* (Feb. 1980), 116-118 ff.

Zhou Liangpei.
"*Huabi xia de zhexue: Kan Kunming Shen She huazhan* (The Philosophy Behind the Brush: A Look at Kunming's Shen She Painting Exhibition)," *Meishu yanjiu 1* (1981), 43; 69-71.

Zhou Ling and Zhou Ping.
Baimiaoji. Tianjin: People's Art Press, 1987.

Zhou Yang.
"Chinese Literature and Art: Our Lessons and Tasks Ahead," *Beijing Review* 22:50 (Dec. 14, 1979), 8-15.

INDEX

ABOUT THE AUTHOR

Ann Barrott Wicks is an associate professor of Asian art history at Miami University in Oxford, Ohio. She received a Ph.D. degree in Oriental Art History from Cornell University in 1982. A specialist in Chinese painting history, Dr. Wicks has published a variety of articles on Qing literati painting and contemporary Chinese painting. She is married to Robert S. Wicks, an expert in Southeast Asian art history. They have three children, Christopher Robert, David Barrott and Elizabeth Mary Ann Wicks.